D1384730

EQUAL PARTNERS

Volume 174   Sage Library of Social Research

RECENT VOLUMES IN . . .
SAGE LIBRARY OF SOCIAL RESEARCH

EQUAL PARTNERS
Successful Women
in Marriage

Dana Vannoy-Hiller
William W. Philliber

Volume 174
SAGE LIBRARY OF
SOCIAL RESEARCH

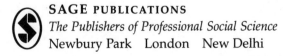

SAGE PUBLICATIONS
The Publishers of Professional Social Science
Newbury Park   London   New Delhi

For information address:

SAGE Publications, Inc.
2111 West Hillcrest Drive
Newbury Park, California 91320

SAGE Publications Ltd.
28 Banner Street
London EC1Y 8QE
England

SAGE Publications India Pvt. Ltd.
M-32 Market
Greater Kailash I
New Delhi 110 048 India

Printed in the United States of America

Library of Congress Cataloging-in-Publication Data

Vannoy-Hiller, Dana.
   Equal partners: successful women in marriage / Dana Vannoy-Hiller and William W. Philliber.
     p. cm.—(Sage library of social research: 174)
   Bibliography: p.
   Includes index.
   ISBN 0-8039-2813-0. — ISBN 0-8039-2814-9 (pbk.)
   1. Dual-career families—United States. 2. Marriage—United States. 3. Wives—Employment—United States. I. Philliber, William W., 1943- . II. Title. III. Series.
HQ536.V37 1989
306.87—dc20
                                 89-33175
                                     CIP

FIRST PRINTING, 1989

Contents

Acknowledgments

We are grateful for the help and support of many people in the preparation of this book. We appreciate very much the support of the National Science Foundation through grant #SES-8121064, which was essential for doing the research reported here. Dana Vannoy-Hiller also received research support from the University Research Council, the Taft Fund, and the Center for the Study of Work and Family—all of the University of Cincinnati.

We wish to thank Daniel Shatzer, research associate, for his competent direction of the data collection; Karen Feinberg for her thorough and sensitive editing of the manuscript; and Marilyn Glass and Cheryl Fuhrmann for timely typing of various drafts of parts of the book. Colleen Nunn typed the final manuscript, and for her attention to detail and careful word processing, we are grateful.

Finally, we appreciate the friendly patience and forbearance of our editor at Sage, Mitch Allen, and the support and encouragement of our friends and families.

Dana Vannoy-Hiller
William W. Philliber

CHAPTER ONE

Sex Equality in Marriage

SEX EQUALITY IN MARRIAGE?

In one-half of all American marriages today, both spouses are employed outside the home (Statistical Abstract, 1986:399). This figure represents a revolution over a relatively short period of time; as recently as 1960 only 25% of wives with husbands present in the home were employed. Some wives are enjoying occupational achievements and/or income comparable to those of their husbands, a situation for which many couples are ill prepared. These couples have been socialized to a set of traditional role expectations that do not match their current objective circumstances. Whether or not they intended it, they are pioneers in a new style of marriage relationship. A second occupational commitment, and perhaps especially a second professional career, imposes new pressures on the role fit of partners that may affect their interaction, communication, and mutual emotional gratification in complex and challenging ways.

We wrote this book to learn something about couples who manage successfully to carry out the demands of two occupations while maintaining a quality relationship in their marriages. We expected that a variety of factors contributed to contemporary marital problems and that the circumstances these factors represent were exacerbated by marriages in which wives achieve in work as highly as their husbands, or even more highly. Couples who succeed in maintaining two jobs as well as good marriages are at the leading edge of a lifestyle change in American society.

We want to emphasize that we are not positing equal occupational or income statuses as the *cause* of marital stress or breakdown, although analysis of current aggregate data would seem to suggest this. Many marriages between partners with equal achievements do survive. It is more accurate to say that such marriages create situations that sift the good relationships from the less good. Marriages of the past lasted until death, but were not necessarily highly successful in regard to quality. The difference in today's marriages is that many of the traditional supports have disappeared, such as the family functioning as an economic unit and being embedded in a kinship network. Marital stability today depends much more strongly on the conjugal relationship, which depends in turn on the partners' capacity for love and acceptance and on their interpersonal skill. The presence of equal breadwinners in a marriage does not cause divorce, but it makes the option a realistic possibility when problems exist in the emotional relationship.

We wish to place this marital phenomenon in a wider picture—the evolution of social structure—and in doing so to underscore the essential interdependence between human personality and social environment. The difficulties encountered in sustaining contemporary marital relationships may be temporal problems resulting from a lack of congruence in the elements of social life. Accordingly we will discuss the social and psychological issues in the marriage relationship associated with the dramatic change in women's economic role over the last three decades. On the basis of findings from a study of 489 married couples conducted in 1982–83, we will attempt to explain who is more or less likely to succeed in the new circumstance of spouses who have relatively equal occupational statuses or earning power.

The purpose of this book is fourfold. First, we intend to call our readers' attention to the relationship between social structure and people's internal beliefs, attitudes, and self-concepts. As the nature of society changes, cultural elements, including members' prototypical attitudes and behaviors, also must change. At some times structure and personalities may be more in equilibrium than at others.

Second, we describe in a general way how society is evolving in a direction that increasingly supports and enhances the possibility of sex equality. From a long view of human history, the social forces shaping the macrostructure of society are weakening patriarchal order.

Third, we wish to suggest that contemporary gender-role issues and widespread marital instability result in part from a lag between structural realities and women's and men's prototypical internal states. To highlight this lack of congruence we focus on marriages in which an external sex equality is most apparent, namely marriages of two independent, self-sustaining earners.

Finally, we study effects of interaction between occupational equality and certain psychological variables in order to determine exactly how marital partners are responding to new circumstances. Specifically, we ask what psychological variables are associated with greater or lesser marital quality in marriages where partners do or do not have equal occupational achievements. In studying these outcomes we control for demographic locations in the wider social structure.

We hope to show the variability of internal adaptation to the present social environment while making it clear that none of us escapes being reshaped by changing social conditions. What happens when spouses are equal breadwinners? This is an important question for the late twentieth century; even if we are not affected, our children will feel the effects.

This chapter discusses the extent and distribution of sex equality, describes the potential problems for couples, and focuses on variables that may help to differentiate those who do from those who do not adapt readily to being equal partners. The intent of Chapter 2 is to indicate the sources of change in the macrostructure of society that support the emerging equality. Chapter 3 provides the social psychological, theoretical background from which our ideas derive. Personal identities, prototypical gender-role identities, are constructed as individuals interact with their social milieu.

Chapters 4, 5, and 6 present findings about marital quality from our study of dual-earner couples. Chapter 4 discusses the relevance of social structural variables; Chapter 5 concerns the importance of the family division of labor and reports spouses' expectations about what the division of labor should be; Chapter 6 addresses the importance of competitiveness, relationship imbalance, and gender-role identity as psychological variables relevant to successful equal-partner marriages. Chapter 7 summarizes our analysis of change and describes the potential for emerging sex equality in marriage.

Aggregate data indicating the extent of change within American marriages is plentiful. During the 1950s American women were mothering the baby boom generation, but by 1980 childbearing had fallen below natural replacement levels. Women's labor-force participation increased from 34% of all women aged 16 to 64 in 1950 to 52% in 1980; 12% of wives with preschool children were employed in 1950, and 50% of those wives were employed in 1980. Now for the first time, more women than men are enrolled in college (Bianchi and Spain, 1983a).

Not only are more wives working; some are the primary breadwinners. Among the 49 million couple households in the civilian population in 1981, the wife earned more than the husband in 5.9 million households, or 12% (Bianchi and Spain, 1983b:7). Among dual-earner couples, 16% of the wives earned more than their husbands and another 2% earned as much. The wife earned twice as much as her husband in 1.6 million, or 6% of the dual-earner couples (Bianchi and Spain, 1983b:14). Thus, in nearly one-fifth of households with both spouses working, wives earn as much as their husbands, or more.[1] In short, we now have a significant number of couples in which earning power does not remain solely with the male head of household. It has been shown that wives who earn are more powerful in their marriages than those who do not, and that those who earn more are even more powerful (Fox and Hesse-Biber, 1984:183; Hood, 1983). Other women may not earn more money than their husbands, but many are in occupations that carry higher social status (Haug, 1973; Watson and Barth, 1964).

Clearly the work lives of American women are changing, and these new circumstances have significant ramifications for married life and for marital stability. The most obvious consequence is that each partner has the economic ability to live independently of the other. In the past, a marriage consisting of two economically independent people would have been extremely rare; women were bound to their husbands out of necessity. Now the family is a consuming unit, and individuals are more often economically self-sufficient. We should emphasize that this self-sufficiency, however, does not imply equality in standard of living or in access to rewards. The occupational sex segregation in the labor force and the overall income differentials between women and men in the economy combine with the traditional expectations regarding women at home to perpetuate the general subordination of women. Roles in the economy and at home must change together to alter women's status. Now that economic self-sufficiency is possible, emotional gratification has become the most important function of the family; this function may be far more difficult for families to fulfill consistently.

The Crux of the Matter

The revolution pulling women into the modern labor force has significant effects for American marriages. As women's access to the more desirable occupations increases, the old traditional role bargains at home are undermined, particularly in proportion to the wife's contribution to family income. The interdependence between married men and women, which was fixed by the specialization of breadwinning and homemaking roles, has been reduced; consequently, marriages which were built mostly on economic considerations are threatened.

Scanzoni and Scanzoni (1981) describe the evolution from the "owner-property" marriage pattern of the eighteenth century to the "head-complement" pattern prevalent throughout much of the twentieth century, the "senior-partner/junior-partner" pattern of the more recent past and the present, and the currently evolving "equal-partner" marriage. In the 1980s most marriages fall somewhere between the traditional head-complement type and the equal-partner type.

When wives were legally the property of husbands, the power relation in the dyad was extremely one-sided. Women exchanged sexual favors and childbearing for board and lodging, and depended completely on their husbands for basic survival. Industrialization brought women an alternative means of survival: jobs, albeit undesirable ones. The very presence of an alternative altered the owner-property relationship, and the typical marriage became a head-complement arrangement. Women came to have more rights; they could expect more understanding and more emotional support from their husbands. Even so, the breadwinner/caretaker division of labor in marriage remained convenient and met the needs of the growing economy.

As women began to assume part of the income-producing role outside the home, the wife's complementary position changed to that of a junior partner. In this pattern the wife is likely to have more power within the relationship. It is still the husband's duty to be the main breadwinner; the wife simply adds an occupational role to her child-care and household responsibilities. Today the great majority of dual-earner couples follow the senior-partner/junior-partner pattern.

The crucial elements in the equal-partner pattern are a strong commitment to work on the part of both spouses and the production of income at near-equal levels. This pattern includes a greater degree of role interchangeability with respect to breadwinning and domestic duties, and the power relationship is likely to be more equal as well. In these marriages women's educational, occupational, and income achievements are more likely to be comparable to their husbands'. The change from a relationship based on the husband's economic dominance to an economically equal relationship between spouses is dramatic because of the deep, widespread, and persistent expectations of male dominance and female submissiveness.

Marriages are subject to additional stress not only because each partner has the opportunity for economic self-sufficiency, but also because the family contains two wage earners in a society organized for single-earner households. The demands of two jobs and of maintaining a household, particularly if children are present, may create a situation in which more competition between the sexes is generated, even less time and less energy are available for nurturing one another, the routines become rigid from necessity, and couples readily play roles rather than relating truly to one another. These problems are never expected, but they are common.

The influx of married women into the labor force in recent decades has added a work role outside the home, typically for low wages, for the vast majority of these women. White wives who are full-time year-round workers earn an average of 25% of their family incomes; their black counterparts earn an average of 33% (Statistical Abstract, 1980). Bianchi and Spain (1983b:4) report that among white families, the average earnings of all working wives increased from 12% to 18% of family earnings between 1959 and 1978. Among black families, the comparable figure rose from 17% to 28%. For most couples the respective proportions of family income earned are still uneven, with the male earning more, but for a growing minority they are approaching equality.

The discussion in this book is meant to generalize to all dual-earner marriages in which partners are at risk of having relatively equal occupational status or relatively equal incomes. The data reported in later chapters are taken from a random sample of couples designed to oversample dual-earner couples, especially dual-earner couples with wives in professional, male sex-typed occupations. This group—dual-earner couples approaching occupational or income equality—conceivably may include couples in the upper middle, middle, or working classes.

The population at risk may be more likely to be upper middle and middle than working class for two reasons. First, even though the potential for income equality among working partners may be similar for all classes (or even greater for the lower middle classes), the potential for two *self-sufficient* incomes is less in the lower middle and working classes. Second, sex segregation of the occupational structure is somewhat more apparent in working-class occupations, where people are employed in blue-collar and pink-collar jobs. We believe that the sex-segregated labor force provides an important buffer for direct occupational comparisons between spouses and that problems are exacerbated when wives are employed in male sex-typed occupations.

The dual-career literature focuses on dual-professional couples and hence makes their lifestyle more visible as a new variant. The heavy demands of professional occupational roles may generate additional pressures on a couple's potential for achieving marital quality, but we believe that the processes and mechanisms discussed here apply across classes whenever independent resources exist to provide realistic alternatives to the marriage.

Dual-professional couples are and will continue to be a very small proportion of the total population, just as professional one-earner families have been a small proportion of the total population until now. *Within* this upper-middle-class segment of American society, however, the number of these couples is likely to increase. Professional men are increasingly marrying professional women rather than unemployed women. Because norms and customs tend to filter down through the class system, these people often are seen as pioneering a new lifestyle. We suspect that there may be pioneers across the class system, who are attempting to create a new lifestyle for two breadwinners while they raise children and attend to the everyday needs of living. The social psychological variables that we have studied should serve as relevant predictors of marital quality for dual-earner couples regardless of social class.

It is a common theme both in the sociological and economics literature (Becker et al., 1977; Hornung and McCullough, 1977; Parsons, 1942) and in the popular press (Rubenstein, 1982; *Wall Street Journal*, 1982) that the wife's occupational or income equivalence or superiority is threatening to the couple's marital happiness. In part this is true simply because such a situation is deviant from the pattern of male superiority that was (and still is) most typical. The situation goes against the mainstream and is contrary to men's dominance in economic institutions and organizations.

The popular press is pessimistic about women's potential to be highly successful both at work and in a marital relationship, and some research data support the popular image. For example, in 1977 women aged 35 to 44 with graduate degrees and personal incomes above $20,000 were four times as likely to divorce as women with lower occupational achievements. In *American Couples,* Blumstein and Schwartz (1983) note that success at work appears to diminish a woman's chances of a successful marriage. Amanda Spake (1984) and Judith Stiehm (1976) discuss the phenomenon in journalistic fashion: Spake describes the role conflict inherent in the lives of high-achieving women, and Stiehm addresses the complications of mate selection.

Spake (1984:48) suggests that marital stress may result from the battle between love and work that takes place within married, career-oriented women. Work-oriented men traditionally are faulted but excused for putting less than the optimum amount of time and energy into their marital relationships. Taking care of the couple usually is the woman's job; in this respect work-centered women are at a disadvantage. Spake says that the new generation of women, who must face the fact that the traditional female role cannot sustain them either emotionally or economically, must develop a new set of qualities to survive in the male-dominated marketplace. These qualities include ambition, competitiveness, assertiveness, and the will to win, but these very qualities can be antithetical to building solid interpersonal relationships between women and men. Traditionally, the qualities important to women for establishing, creating, and sustaining long-term relationships with men have been cooperation, nurturance, and the impulse to yield. Men, society, and even women themselves still expect women to embody these qualities. Women's and men's present difficulties in achieving intimacy, Spake suggests, probably are aggravated by conflicts caused by the schism between the new realities and the old expectations.

On another note, Stiehm (1976) explains how the "invidious intimacy" in many successful women's marriages has helped to sustain those marriages. She points out that women who do not fear success have something important in common—an intimate relationship with a man they believe to be smarter, and hence, at least potentially, more successful. Stiehm (1976:12) says, "These women, then, can afford to achieve because their men will achieve more. Their excellence will not threaten the traditional invidious relationship between female and male intimates. To be brief, successful women seem to position themselves carefully so that their public success will not create private cost." This theme is not unusual; other scholars have written in a similar vein (Holstrom, 1973; Kundsin, 1974).

Stiehm makes the interesting point that *only by trying* do most men and most women enter a relationship that suggests regularly and visibly that women require someone to take care of them. She notes that (1) if pairing were random, the woman would be taller than the man in one out of six couples, but people studiously avoid this situation; (2) there is more weight variation among men than between the average man and the average woman, so couples must pair selectively to avoid wives outsizing husbands; (3) most marriages are contracted between older men and younger women; (4) the best-educated men marry women with less or sometimes equal education, while the best-educated women marry men with more or sometimes equal education; and, of course, (5) the great majority of men earn greater incomes than their wives; this difference is greatest at the higher levels. So tall, mature, well-educated, high-income, high-status women conventionally ally themselves with taller, older, better-educated, wealthier, higher-status men!

Stiehm raises several interesting questions about the implications of this tendency. Does this pattern of "invidious intimacy" lead to lesser self-esteem, underaccomplishment, or underrecognition of women? Does it cause wives to defer unconsciously to husbands? Does it cripple them for rigorous competition? And what of the men? When wives who are only slightly lesser by conventional measures of success also make essential contributions to their husbands' professional and personal well-being, how can their husbands accept them as professional equals? To do so would require acknowledging that women can do alone what men can do only with considerable help. Is it the apparent necessity for this widespread and common invidious intimacy that explains women's failure to win distinction in the public realm?

These commentaries suggest that successful women must either sacrifice marriage or pair up with even more successful men. One need not be a mathematician to see that not many women can be highly successful in both work and marriage if their respective husbands are required to be more successful in work than they. Men's achievements apparently provide a ceiling for their wives' achievements. If this is true, the underlying message is that in American society we have a long way to go toward real acceptance of sex equality both in the economy and in marriage.

The Importance of Relative Occupational Status

Wealth, prestige, and power are important social rewards in American society. Generally these rewards are correlated highly and are distributed according to one's function in society: that is, according to occupation. Whether or not we wish it to be so, occupational status (with the accompanying educational requirements and monetary benefits) is a significant means of comparing people in society. Occupation reflects the individual's power and determines the respect accorded to him or her. Although the subject is less often discussed openly, these indicators (occupational status, income, and education) also can reflect one's power and the respect accorded to one in a marital relationship. The spouses' relative occupational achievements provide an objective index of status equality or the lack of it. As the achievements become more similar, the situation violates the common expectation of male dominance not only in the marriage relationship, but also in the public realm outside the family. Some people are more able than others to tolerate the costs of such nonconformity.

The research evidence specifically concerning spouses' relative occupational statuses and marital stress and/or dissolution is somewhat mixed. On the one hand, some theorists (Becker et al., 1977; Santos, 1975) suggest that similar occupational achievement on the part of spouses decreases the necessary complementarity in their roles; others show that considerable inequality in occupational achievements in either direction (Hornung and McCullough, 1977) are related to marital difficulties. On the other hand, some researchers have found no evidence that women drop out of the labor force or their marriages to avoid competing with their husbands (Oppenheimer, 1977); in fact, the occupational status that the wife can expect to achieve is a major factor in determining her participation in the labor force (Hiller and Philliber, 1980). Still others (Richardson, 1979; Simpson and England, 1982) have found no evidence that marital satisfaction diminishes when the wives' occupational achievements exceed those of their husbands.

In 1983 we studied a subsample of 984 working women from the National Longitudinal Survey to determine whether marital dissolution or other negative outcomes occur in marriages in which wives have equal or superior achievements (Philliber and Hiller, 1983). When we examined spouses' occupational characteristics in 1967 and then noted the changes in marriages and/or jobs in 1974, we found that the wife's employment in a job usually held by a man predicted later negative changes. Women in such jobs were more likely to become divorced, to leave the labor force, or to move to a lower-status job than women in jobs usually held by women. These women were also very likely to shift to jobs sex-typed as female. The relative occupational prestige of the two spouses contributed to the probability of these changes, but the effects of prestige were not as large as those of the sex type of the wife's occupation. We concluded that a wife's employment in a position traditionally occupied by men may provide for a direct comparison of achievements, a situation which is avoided when wives hold positions traditionally occupied by women.

Research conducted by Hornung et al. (1981) indicates that 1) there is more mutual physical and verbal abuse in two-earner families; 2) there is more actual violence when the wife's occupational status is higher than the husband's; and 3) the husband's mortality rate increases as the wife's job status increases relative to the husband's.

Finally, women with five or more years of college have much higher marital disruption rates than women with only four years of college; this disruption increases if the women were married before beginning graduate school rather than after (Houseknecht and Macke, 1981; Houseknecht and Spanier, 1980).[2] These findings and our own seem to indicate that marriages in which wives' occupational achievements are equal or superior to their husbands' may indeed be more difficult to sustain than those in which they are not. This conclusion led us to ask why this might be so and to search for the important intervening variables that may determine success or failure in such marriages.

Toward an Explanation of Marital Stress

Researchers have studied marital stability and marital quality for many years. Of course, variables at the level of the spouses' intimate interaction, such as similar values, emotional gratification, effective communication, and companionship, have been found to be critical. It is likely that these variables can explain a great deal of the variation in marital quality, and do so most directly. Relative occupational status, income, and education, which affect dual-earner couples particularly, exist at a higher level of abstraction and are likely to affect the marital relation, at least in part, by affecting the above dyadic, interpersonal factors; in turn, these factors affect the relationship.

Explanations based upon socioeconomic and life cycle variables have often been used to shed light upon family conflicts and relationships. Without doubt many conflicts between families center around economic issues (Scanzoni and Scanzoni, 1981), and styles of behavior related to education and occupational positions no doubt affect the resolution of those conflicts. However, neither socioeconomic nor life cycle variables seem very powerful predictors of the quality of marriage (Bahr et al., 1983; Huber and Spitze, 1980). Of particular importance, the relative attainment of husbands and wives, in and of itself, seems unimportant (Oppenheimer, 1977; Richardson, 1979).

Sociologists have offered more social psychological explanations for marital distress and/or instability, which seem to assume special significance when considered in light of women's increasing participation in the labor force. These theories emphasize concepts and conditions that may result from or be affected by the extent of status comparison in the marital relationship. They include (1) congruence between role expectations and performance (Mason and Bumpass, 1975; Osmond and Martin, 1975; Parelius, 1975); (2) competition between partners (Barber, 1956; Parsons, 1942; 1943); (3) lack of role complementarity (Becker et al., 1977; Santos, 1975); and (4) threat to gender-role identity (Safilios-Rothschild, 1975).

Congruence Between Role Expectations and Performance

One explanation of marital stress in the research literature is that problems result when partners do not perform marital roles in a manner matching their spouses' or their own expectations. The expectations usually are those apparent in the traditional, normative gender roles of American society. In the 1960s, studies indicated that marital happiness was greatest in traditional relationships in which husbands performed the central provider role. In the 1970s, the research emphasized changing role expectations and performance. Women's attitudes were shifting toward more egalitarian role expectations (Mason and Bumpass, 1975; Mason et al., 1976; Parelius, 1975), but men's attitudes were moving less in this direction (Komarovsky, 1973; Osmond and Martin, 1975). Some researchers concluded that men's expectations also shifted but that women did not perceive this shift and thus experienced strain from adopting attitudes they believed men would reject (Parelius, 1975).

Both women and men still tend to behave traditionally. Most wives still do most of the household work and view their labor-market activity as having a job in order to "help out." By the same token, men occasionally "help out" at home but rarely feel responsible. It is unclear, however, whether women's and men's role expectations differ or whether the difference is only perceived. It is not known whether incongruence between role expectations and perceptions of performance are the cause of difficulties when the wife's occupational achievements equal or surpass her husband's.

Competition Between Partners

Talcott Parsons (1942; 1943) was one of the first sociologists to write about wives as well as husbands having occupational achievements. He believed that if both spouses were employed, their achievements might lead to judgments about who was more successful. Spouses would be in competition with one another, and this competition would be disruptive to the marriage. In Parsons' view, competition could be prevented if the wife's achievements were consistent with normative expectations about the primacy of her homemaking role and if she did not seek status rewards from her own job but rather derived those rewards from her husband's job. We know that conflict occurs in many cases in which the wife's achievements are equal to or greater than her husband's, but we do not know specifically whether the conflict is a result of actual competition between the spouses.

Lack of Role Complementarity

In a traditional relationship, where the husband is the key provider and the wife is the key performer of housekeeping roles, roles are complementary; the relationship is balanced in that each partner is more powerful in areas that are important to the other. If the wife develops a successful career and if other roles remain unchanged, however, she is less dependent on her husband than he on her; the relationship is unbalanced. Stress is created for her because she contributes more to the relationship than she receives, and for him because he is the more dependent partner. Becker et al. (1977) found that an increase in men's expected earnings reduced the probability of a marital dissolution, while an increase in women's expected earnings increased the probability. It could be that a perceived imbalance in contribution to the relationship causes marital stress.[3]

Threat to Gender-Role Identity

Gender, unlike biological sex, is a social construction, the culturally defined behavioral expectations for women and for men. Gender is referred to as *feminine* or *masculine,* and gender-role identity refers to the extent to which a woman or a man incorporates traditional feminine and/or masculine role definitions into his or her self-concept. Gender roles are interwoven intricately with social status such that women traditionally have had a subordinate role and men a superordinate role. To gain social status in the wider community, a woman has had to marry well by attracting a good provider with her feminine charms. Concomitantly, a man's status can be displayed by the attractiveness of the woman under his care and by how well he provides for her (Safilios-Rothschild, 1975).

Social scientists who study social status usually have not examined gender identity. Theorists so far have not considered the possibility that when a woman chooses to achieve in the labor force and if her ability to do so is equivalent to or greater than her husband's, she jeopardizes some of the status she might otherwise receive from appearing able to attract a high-status husband. Her sexual attractiveness or femininity becomes suspect. Likewise, when a man's wife holds a higher-status position or earns more than he does, he may share in the prestige of added income and even of her occupation, but his ability to be the provider is questioned.

Several social scientists have discussed how the breadwinner's role validates a man's masculinity (Gronseth, 1972; Pleck, 1977; Yankelovich, 1974). Particularly for men whose jobs are not inherently satisfying psychologically, daily work is worthwhile because the sacrifices they make to provide for their families validate them as men. If a man values highly a traditional masculine gender-role identity, including being the family provider and having the privileges of that role, he may become uncomfortable in a relationship where he is not the sole provider. Similarly, being cared for by a man and providing at the same time for his daily needs can help validate a woman's femininity. If a woman values highly a traditional feminine gender-role identity, including playing a supportive and subordinate role to significant males, she may become uncomfortable in a relationship in which she appears to herself or to others to be exerting dominance, such as when her occupational attainment surpasses her husband's. In both cases the trappings of traditional sex stratification are important to the individual's self-concept.

It seems reasonable that when the wife's occupational attainment surpasses the husband's, the situation may pose a threat to the husband's gender-role identity if the masculine role is an important part of his self-concept and to the wife's identity if the feminine role is very significant for her self-concept.

In the 1970s, researchers (e.g., Bem, 1974) began to describe a third gender-role identity, androgyny. Psychological androgyny is a blend of feminine and masculine characteristics. Block (1973) used the term to describe gender-role behaviors beyond typical female-male differences, representing a successful balancing of agency and communion. When both partners tend to have androgynous gender-role identities—that is, when they are comfortable with both the masculine and the feminine elements in their personalities—it seems reasonable that they may adjust more readily to the wife's occupational achievements equaling or surpassing the husband's.

GENDER, POWER, AND STATUS

The balance of power is the element that has changed most dramatically in some marital role bargains. As exemplified in the Scanzoni and Scanzoni (1981) typology discussed earlier, this balance is moving from extreme one-sidedness to greater equality. The balance of power appears to be correlated highly with each partner's access to resources necessary for survival outside the marriage. When the husband is in a position to mediate his wife's access to these resources, he is more powerful. When both partners have direct access, the power in the relationship is more balanced.

Social and Psychological Power

Today, an analysis of social structure indicates that men hold the significant positions of power. It is useful to remember that the social structures that gender role patterns represent are not "intended" by individuals. Although individuals monitor their behavior and direct it toward their own goals and purposes, there is no direct, intentional connection between individual purposes and the form that social structure takes. The latter is the result of preexisting forms as they are reproduced daily by both the intended and the unintended activities of individuals. The changing balance of power in marriage occurs through the specific activities and negotiations of real individuals who have their own purposes. Yet at the social level of analysis, the balance results from major shifts in the economic and demographic structure of society.

At the social level of analysis the source of power can be seen readily in economic and demographic terms. These are the leading determinants of the setting for marriage partners. The availability of employment for women, and in fact the demand for it, has been extremely important in changing marital role bargains. In an analysis of the implications of the sex ratio, Guttentag and Secord (1983) make the major point that social roles are not only a reflection of internalized norms, but in fact emerge and are maintained by the distribution of power among interacting individuals. When the dyadic balance of power between women and men (with respect to sex ratio) shifts, social roles are likely to change as well. Although social norms may be internalized, they must be supported continually by the existing relationships and the behaviors of real people.

At the social psychological level of analysis, emotional power, described in terms of emotional dependence and independence between partners, is also a consideration. Rubin (1983:126) explains how men's economic independence has been mistaken for emotional independence, and how women's economic dependence has led us to assume that they are emotionally dependent as well. From early in their lives, males are urged to be independent: to be free, self-sufficient, and in command. Females do not universally desire independence but generally grow up to fear it; they are more concerned about being nurtured and not being alone. Thus, independence has been valued in men, not in women. Although women seek dependence and men independence, Rubin (1983:122) says that "things are not always what they seem." She asked her male respondents to pretend that something had happened to their wives, and then asked if they would want to marry again. Nearly all said yes without hesitation. They knew that women in their lives provided comfort, support, and nurturance. When Rubin asked her female respondents the same question, nearly half said they would not marry again, particularly those who had been married longer and had no children left in the home. A significant proportion of women regarded marriage as having at least as many costs as benefits.

Because women are less valued than men even in youth but particularly by midlife, and because they are less likely to find partners at that point, the circumstances they face are very different from those faced by men. Widowhood is difficult for both women and men, and yet a woman's life span is not affected by her husband's death if she stays single. The same is not true of men; they may be in jeopardy if they do not remarry (Kund et al., 1981; Susser, 1981). In general, research shows that married men are healthier and live longer than single men, but that the reverse is true for women. The ideology that insists that women are the dependent sex, says Rubin (1983:128), blinds us to the evidence showing otherwise.

Rubin suggests that men depend on women for something more fundamentally important than physical care. Women provide not only stability but a means for emotional expression that is unavailable elsewhere in most men's lives. Women have friends, not merely workmates or colleagues, and the content and quality of their friendships are deeper than those of men. In Rubin's own study of friendship she found that single women had no problem identifying best friends, usually other women. A large majority of single men, however, could not name a best friend; if they did so, it was more likely to be a woman than a man. Among married persons, far more men than women named their spouse. If a woman named her spouse, it was likely to be in conjunction with another trusted friend. Women friends share intimacies and emotional support, while men friends are likely to share activities and experiences.

"The ideology of the dependent woman and the independent man," says Rubin, "is maintained because of the barriers in social arrangements which prevent women's independence and men's dependence." Women are both economically and socially disadvantaged in comparison to men; norms insist that passivity and dependence are the core of femininity, and because a woman is known and judged in the community according to the man in her life, it is important for her, as well as for him, to believe that he is the stronger. If he shows his vulnerabilities she may become ambivalent, even hostile, toward him. Men sense this possibility and resist dropping their guard.

Rubin says that a complex relationship exists between economic and emotional dependency, and that for any adult a prolonged and profound economic dependency will become an emotional dependency as well. A woman in this circumstance experiences herself as she did when she was a child, and, like a child, she will try to comply with the powerful parent's expectations.

Rubin finds this self-fulfilling prophesy distressing. In sum, our ideology calls out behavior both in women and in men which reinforces the ideology so that it seems like truth, although in reality none of us can quite match the stereotypes. In actual fact, the mutual emotional dependency that women and men often experience is symbiotic; neither sex is quite whole without the other.

Gender roles are interwoven with social status in complex and intricate ways. Traditionally a woman could, and still can, achieve or maintain a degree of social status by marrying well; to do this she must attract a high-status man. Exhibiting typical feminine charms, especially physical attractiveness, is highly relevant to her success in this venture. If she is too assertive or too competent she may lose some of her beguiling dependency and lessen her chances for success in the matching process. On the other hand, a man's social standing, as represented by successful achievements, often is made apparent to others by the attractiveness of the woman he is able to attract and the degree of luxury in which he keeps her.

If women and men deviate from this traditional exchange by allowing the woman to exhibit equal or even superior achievements, one or both may feel that their gender-role identity—their masculinity or femininity—is threatened. The threat is that one may lose the personal social status derived from association with an appropriately conforming partner. The man risks being seen as "less of a man" because his wife can do things he can do and is not helplessly dependent on him; the woman risks being seen as "less of a woman" because she has not been able to attract a man who is superior to her in achievements. One can imagine the lack of passion that would most likely exist in a relationship in which partners were not pleased with their own self-concepts. In such cases, the structure of traditional sex stratification in one's intimate relationship is an important support to the partners' identities or self-concepts. The head-complement and the senior-partner/junior-partner marriage role bargains fit the traditional model of male-female relationships, but the equal-partner/equal-partner marriage pattern does not. This new marriage bargain presents new challenges for the partners, which concern important identity issues.

Gender-role identity is part of the self-concept that develops over several years; it may or may not change to varying degrees over a lifetime, depending on specific life experiences. Such changes are associated strongly with changes in the external social environment of each individual. When change affects whole cohorts of women and men, a society experiences a normative change that can be measured and identified. Are there appreciable differences between 1955 and 1985, for example, in the proportions of men who are comfortable with diapering babies, doing the family grocery shopping, or communicating their need for emotional support; or in the proportions of women who are comfortable in working on road crews, speaking to large political gatherings, or purchasing stocks and bonds? As the societal definitions of appropriate roles for women and men are modified, some individuals are more able than others, by virtue of their personal experiences and the expectations of people significant to them, to let go of old expectations or take on new expectations as part of their self-concepts.

The traditional marital relationship assumes a status difference between the man and the woman, which is provided by the sex stratification of the wider society. That difference is incorporated into the individual's identity as part of the masculine or feminine self-image. If real circumstances alter this difference and if gender-role identities are not altered in a parallel manner, one or both partners will suffer discomfort.

Implications for Marital Bargains

Masculine and feminine gender-role expectations associated with spousal roles are interdependent clusters of norms, and when we incorporate those role expectations into our self-concepts we adopt the whole role set. If our partner's role performance is incongruent with what we expect and does not complement our own performance, we may question our own identity;

hence we are uncomfortable in the relationship. Specifically, if our gender-role identity requires that we have more or less status than our partner, we will feel uncomfortable if this is not the case.

Rapoport and Rapoport (1971; 1975) used the concept of "identity tension line" in defining how far marriage partners will go toward establishing new identities more congruent with those of their partners. The line is the point at which discomfort arises for an individual, at which further experimenting with either nonconventional or traditional behavior would disturb one's self-esteem. Partners' identity tension lines can be seen as the temporary structural givens in a relationship; they serve as warnings of sensitive areas of resistance, or of areas where consciousness raising is needed. For a man, tension lines that represent greater acceptance of androgyny may include the amount of responsibility he can take for detailed domestic chores, as distinct from "helping out," or whether he can tolerate his wife's earning more than he earns; for a woman, these lines may determine just how far she will let herself go in relation to higher-level career opportunities (if they exist), or whether she can tolerate her husband's being praised for his cooking at a dinner party.

These tension lines cannot be avoided or denied, but must be worked out if marital quality is to be achieved by couples who want to self-actualize and to express themselves in a more gender-balanced fashion. They must be discussed; the partners' feelings must be acknowledged. Once acknowledged, the feelings are likely to lose some of their power. Many people feel trapped by gender-role expectations that their spouses communicate, and which the spouses may have learned early in their own lives. Some of these are very obvious: husbands who do not want wives to work outside the home or to play a better game of golf, and wives who push husbands to work aggressively for promotions or who do not want them to appear too shy or too solicitous. Other expectations may be much less obvious, but they are present and they are felt. Spouses should be conscious of their own identity tension lines and those of their partners.

Many people have spoken to us about their attempts to estab-

lish more egalitarian relationships. Their observations and experiences, given below, suggest the variety in identity tension lines
and show how they may be expressed in relationships. The
names are fictitious.

Sue Jansen, an economist, is married to a high-level corporate
manager. She has a Ph.D., but works only part time offering
business seminars. Sue says that her husband is very proud of
the fact that she is bright, but he likes her as a dilettante, not as a
professional person. To acquaintances Bob Jansen appears sensitive and self-assured, but when her clients call for Dr. Jansen, he
makes jokes about the title. In her view, he belittles any involve-
ments on her part that border on real professional activities. One
wonders whether it would be possible for Sue to take a full-time
position and still remain married to Bob.

Carol Smithe, a professor of foreign languages and cultures,
is married to an engineer who is somewhat less subtle. Carol is
employed full time. Although her husband, Mike, appears to be
thankful for her employment, he takes every opportunity to
speak about the "esoteric" and, therefore, unimportant, en-
deavor in which she engages as well as the small size of her
paycheck. He makes these comments in front of friends and
family.

Men as well as women are confronted with the expectations
that exist and the feelings that result when they are not met.
Barbara Worthy, an administrative secretary, was married to Sam
Worthy, a sales manager who was also an avid gardener, a gour-
met cook, and a doting father. Sam spent a great deal of leisure
time with his children. He did not like the pressure of the corporation. Finally he decided he hated his job and quit. Eventually
he decided to earn a certificate to teach in junior high school. In
the meantime, his wife left him. She said the family did not need
a cook and a gardener but someone who wanted to achieve
something in life.

In some situations the tension lines may be even more subtle.
Karen Haines, a clinical psychologist, is married to Ralph, a Ph.D.
physicist working in a corporation. Ralph genuinely encourages
her achievement and is seen by others as especially sensitive, but

Karen says he seems to feel upstaged whenever she shows any sign of professional expertise in a social situation. If the conversation relates to her field or her professional activities, he redirects the discussion at the first opportunity. If friends ask her about psychological topics and she responds, particularly if she risks an explanation, Ralph may start a debate or suggest that she is biased. Later, in private, he accuses her of lecturing and acting as if she has the final word, and suggests that she sharpen her interpersonal skills. Karen is learning that to please her husband in social conversation, she must not draw attention to herself, particularly in her professional role. Being well informed, entertaining, and interesting about subjects other than her field is all right, however. She also realizes that she pleases him by being an expert listener and by drawing out others, a familiar feminine role expectation. She is to appear bright and competent, but apparently not too bright or too competent.

Harry Cresap is a lathe operator, and his wife Julie is a beautician in a city salon. Julie has been saving as much of her income as possible to begin her own beauty shop in their suburb. She has ambitions of owning a good business one day. She also urges Harry to apply for any foreman positions that appear, but he never does so. Such a responsibility does not interest him. Harry resents Julie's skimping to save and he is reluctant to help her in realizing her goal. He likes to go to ballgames and invest in his hobby of racing model cars. Julie feels frustrated by Harry's indifference to getting ahead. It remains to be seen if Harry and Julie will be able to negotiate compromises accepting of each other and each other's projects.

A final example concerns Marcia Acker, who earns a large income as an interior designer. Her husband, Karl, is an attorney whose behavior often does not fit the male stereotype. Although Marcia is grateful for the freedom he allows her, she has hinted at her dismay about her husband's lack of financial success; he earns less than she. Because she also believes that she carries most of the burdens at home, occasionally she feels frustrated and short-changed. Sometimes she questions her need for the relationship. Karl could balance out the costs and the rewards for her by taking over more of the household work and child care, but he seems unlikely to do so. While Marcia may fantasize about a partner with higher status and income, she also recognizes that such a person may need more wifely support than her own professional commitment would allow. Like many women meeting midlife in the current decades, she wants things both ways. Karl probably feels some insecurities about her expectations and consequently discloses less of his own feelings than he might otherwise.

Identity tension lines are drawn in different places and expressed in different ways. In the Jansens' case, the husband is very generous in public; he has no reason not to be, because publicly his wife presents little challenge. He makes his cutting remarks in private. In the case of the Smithes, the wife is employed professionally, and her husband continually finds it necessary to make that employment seem of little importance. Barbara Worthy could not allow her husband to do what he wanted most to do because it appeared to be a lesser achievement than she required in her husband. The example of the Haineses suggests partners who are able to accept a great deal of equality in their lifestyle, but the tension line for the husband appears in social situations in which traditional status impressions are more comfortable for him. Unless the Cresaps can openly discuss and accept each other's desires for the future, they are likely to be on a collision course. Finally, Marcia Acker finds it difficult to tolerate what she considers her superior achievements and a heavier overall workload than her husband's, but she also recognizes the freedom that her spouse allows her. In all six cases the tension lines are felt but repressed. When these spouses do not face their feelings and talk about them openly, the feelings sneak out. Spouses who feel discomfort subconsciously find ways to put the onus on their partners, and they communicate to them that they are the ones not measuring up in traditional terms.

There are interesting interactions between how we evaluate our levels of performance in significant areas and our ability to be close to other people, whether friends or lovers. Our behavior in any relationship, new or well established, is affected by the strategies we use to protect our egos. When the interest or activity is very important to a person's self-concept, that person tends to associate with others who perform well in that activity, but not a great deal better. To do so would diminish the person's self-esteem. For better or for worse, we do not associate with others whose capabilities in significant areas differ widely from our own.

Tesser and his colleagues propose that people prefer associates who do very well on tasks irrelevant to their own sense of self, allowing them to enjoy some of the reflected glory, but who do less well than themselves on tasks central to their own self-concepts, allowing them to maintain self-esteem (Tesser, 1980; Tesser and Campbell, 1980; Tesser and Smith, 1980). This tendency may be even more problematic in relationships where all the trappings of gender-role expectations are also relevant. Because generally we do not expect men to be as good as women at certain things, and vice versa, it is doubly surprising and threatening when they are. If one's partner is not only a friend but a lover or spouse as well, one must be very secure to tolerate that person's superior performance in an activity sex-typed for the opposite sex. If it is more threatening to self-esteem to be outperformed on a task relevant to one's self-definition when one is outperformed by a friend than by a stranger, the potential for problems with spouses is apparent. However, such comparison or competition has no place in an intimate relationship. Partners need to be accepted for themselves, both for their good and their less good qualities. Partners also need to provide support and encouragement for one another.

Today many men seek highly capable mates in terms of whatever qualities they value—intellect, leadership, interpersonal skill—but very few are willing for these mates to be so capable that the men live in their shadows. Increasingly, the same can be said of women. Women have always searched for men whom they perceived as more capable than themselves (Stiehm, 1976), but today a substantial proportion of women are less willing to live so completely in their mates' shadows. On the other hand, women want men who are sensitive and willing to share the raising of the children and the dirty work around the house (Virginia Slims, 1980), but they are less likely to be willing to support househusbands. When a man's wife is highly capable in an occupational role, probably it is easier if that role is different from his own. The comparisons are less direct. Conversely, when a husband is a superb cook or a great decorator, it helps if cooking and decorating are not key sources of self-esteem for his wife.

Both power and status comparisons are important in marriage relationships. Although status resources often are related to power in a relationship, power is a different issue. Many factors, economic and emotional, define the balance of power in marriages. Power defines who is more or less dependent on the relationship. A couple achieves equity when both partners perceive the costs and the rewards of the relationship to be a fair exchange. In such a case both partners feel that they receive sufficient rewards from the relationship for what they invest in it. If the power balance is to be approximately even rather than skewed, both partners must have options; they must be sufficiently independent to have a choice about the relationship. For this reason the changing status of women in postindustrial societies is certainly relevant to the rate of marital dissolution. The traditional balance of costs and rewards is no longer a given.

Status differences between partners are a second source of difficulty; this is a relatively new phenomenon that has emerged with social differentiation and individuation. In communal, agrarian societies gross status differences existed between whole classes, and relatively few marriages took place across those class lines. Statuses were givens and marriage partners shared them. Today, however, social status has a variety of dimensions and is achieved more individually. Statuses associated with occupation provide a continuum, rather than a set of castelike categories. Finally, husbands and wives themselves are seen more as individuals; therefore, the potential for differences between them is greater. Healthy human beings need to feel good about themselves; consequently, status comparisons in one's most intimate relationship must satisfy both partners.

NOTES

1. The more "equal" incomes are more likely to be found in the lower middle classes. Typically the higher the husband's salary, the smaller the wife's salary as a proportion of his (Fox and Hesse-Biber, 1984:183).

2. There is no way to know what is causal in this relationship. Women may enter graduate school and then may experience marital strife, or they may be experiencing marital strife and consequently may enter graduate school.

3. The Parsonian theory about competition between spouses and Becker's theory about complementarity of roles are structural interpretations, whereas we are dealing with attitudes or behaviors of individuals. Thus, in our hypotheses, we make a jump to perceptions of reality regarding competition in the marital relationship and one's sense of satisfaction with the balance in that relationship. This psychological approach is different from the original theoretical formulations, but is closely related.

CHAPTER TWO

Sources of Social Change

Early in this century William F. Ogburn (1966 [1922]) wrote simply but profoundly about the correlation among parts of culture. He proposed that a variety of social problems, as well as the extent of neuroses and some functional psychoses, ultimately were attributable to the inharmonious adjustment of all parts of culture in a period of change. The disharmony occurred when the parts of the whole were out of balance.

The difficulty of maintaining more egalitarian marriages is a problem of harmonious adjustment between the emerging requirements of the macrostructure, on the one hand, and the behaviors and attitudes of women and men, particularly within the marital relationship, on the other. This chapter focuses on the changing characteristics of the macrostructure which are particularly relevant for the decline of sex stratification and for the emerging condition of American marriage. In the first section we discuss social individuation and its relevance for gender roles and the family. The second section describes the larger process of societal evolution of which social individuation is an important element. The next two sections focus directly on the implications of demographic, technological, and economic changes for women's and men's routine behaviors. The fifth section addresses the changing ideologies about sex stratification which have accompanied the new developments in social structure.

SOCIAL INDIVIDUATION

Differentiation is a social trend that motivates and accompanies other elements in societal evolution. It results in the multiplication of social roles or in the increased specialization of functions and activities. Differentiation has increased as society has modernized; as a concurrent development, the individual rather than the group tends to be the source and the goal of social activity. Social differentiation is a division of labor in society, which places human beings in unique positions in relation to others. In such a situation the individual can become increasingly conscious of himself or herself as an individual. In this book we call that process *social individuation*.[1]

In hunting and gathering societies individuals were identified closely with their primary group, and there was less individuality. Tribal members were similar in status, in the roles they played, and in the values they held. Even much later, in horticultural and agrarian societies, social stability and the welfare of the whole were more important than the individual's rights or freedom. For many years this ideology sustained a highly rigid social order which helped assure the survival of the species (Blumberg, 1978). Social order was maintained by the persistence of custom, which was internalized by society's members and by the ascription of certain statuses to individuals. The integrative force was sentiment: love, duty, loyalty toward the proper arrangement of things and fear of the consequences of deviating from that arrangement. Severe sanction was significant for knitting the social fabric more tightly. This "proper arrangement" endured for one's life. In addition, one had little choice about one's role; whether one was to be a peasant, a merchant, or a prince was established at birth.

Today, however, the integrative force of society is a functional interdependence. We need each other's special skills and occupational functions to survive as communities and as nations. As a result, in today's larger, more complex, rapidly changing societies life is freer from coercion and obligation than in the past. Social roles now are more achieved than ascribed; as a result, individuals have become more independent and more self-reliant. Because individuals have more choice about their roles and relationships, these arrangements are defined more often by contract than by traditional expectations. People enter arrangements of mutual dependence, which endure only as long as the parties are agreeable. Marriage has begun to be treated similarly, more as a contractual relationship than as a sacred commitment.

Rationalization, another characteristic of modernization associated with differentiation, represents the increasing value of logic and efficiency over tradition. Differentiation and rationalization have progressed together with change in the scale of human society, from small community to large society, from rural to urban living. As economic production processes were rationalized, specialization in work roles developed. Industrialization broke down the earlier social order, in which the roles were much the same for all men as for all women. For men the diversity of livelihood pursuits increased steadily, but women remained the caretakers of families. Men did the productive work in the outside world; they formed contractual relationships defined by a rational exchange between parties. Meanwhile, women did the maintenance work of providing for the basic human needs of all family members; their relationships continued to be defined by duty.

Paradoxically, the societal trend of role differentiation is responsible for an emerging similarity between women's and men's roles today. It supports a growing sex equality. The ascription of roles to categories of people, including the two sexes, has become wasteful of human resources and dysfunctional for society and for the individual. In industrial nations women are sufficiently well educated to demand a more balanced participation in public and in domestic life. Such a demand is supported by effective control over the timing and number of births. It is increasingly apparent, however, that equality in the public domain ultimately requires newly defined relationships between women and men in marriage and in the family.

Social forces have set the stage for a more differentiated, more rationalized, and, hence, more individualized world, but many people living in postindustrial society still hold to traditional norms for uniformity of women's and men's behavior. This phenomenon is not unusual; human beings rarely change their attitudes until they experience life from a new perspective. For an increasing number of people the new experience of two jobs in a marriage, especially two jobs of equal value, is providing that new perspective. The reality experienced by these people clashes with the old ideas and with the childhood socialization that they are likely to have received.

Our personal identity and our place in the world are validated through interaction with those people with whom we have close, continuing relationships. We really have no identity outside the context of specific social and cultural conditions (Sarbin and Scheibe, 1983:8). We are faced constantly and continuously with the necessity of locating ourselves in relation to others. Marriage is an especially important identity-building relationship; in fact, validating personal identity is an unstated goal of marriage (Berger and Kellner, 1964). We marry to provide structure, stability, and identity in our lives, so it is no wonder that the more flexible expectations existing today cause confusion and conflict.

The gender roles and marital roles that were functional in agrarian times are becoming less so with growing modernization. In complex urban society, individuals now can secure sustenance and can survive as individuals. In many marriages there are two earners—two partners, each with some economic independence. This is the first time in human history in which the marriage relationship has been so free of economic determinism; this fact alone dramatically changes the structure of the relationship.

It is no accident that on the one hand, as more people become economically self-sufficient, they are more likely to be conscious of their individuality; on the other hand, the primary function of marriage and the family is moving from economic production to the satisfaction of the members' needs for closeness and emotional gratification. These shifts are related and have a similar source, the continuing social differentiation. The abundance of personal growth and fulfillment programs, marriage encounters, courses in interpersonal communication, and books on awareness and expression of feelings represents a response to the needs of self-actualizing individuals both as individuals and as family members concerned about family functioning and stability in a new, more atomized world.

The divorce rate, too, should not be surprising; it reflects the confusion of our times. Emile Durkheim (1933), a nineteenth-century social philosopher, proposed that cultural bonds of shared norms, values, and sentiments are less powerful as binding, integrative forces for society than are the social bonds of interdependence in a division of labor. The functional division of labor imposes a system of necessity, while the shared sentiments of individuals are more likely to be influential than absolutely essential. Durkheim was referring to the drift away from the normative homogeneity of rural society and family and toward the more functional integration of individuals in urban society.

While society as a whole has moved toward increasing complexity and functional interdependence, paradoxically the institution of the family has changed in the opposite direction. It has lost the functional interdependence of complementary roles and now must rely more on sentiment—the shared interests, values, and love of its members—for stability. Although this change may render the family less powerful, it also emphasizes the family's greatest significance and strength. The process of social differentiation has made our world more complex and more interdependent, but it has made gender roles less important and has reduced the functions of the family primarily to the support and nurturing of its members.

SOCIETAL EVOLUTION

The process of social differentiation takes place within the context of the evolution of society; across time and space human beings have lived in a great variety of circumstances. The economic activities in which people engage to sustain themselves are the most influential types of behavior for shaping the rest of the social order. Accordingly, sociologists have developed a typology of societies based on the predominant sustenance-getting activity in each society, which is related, of course, to the society's level of technological development. The four basic types are hunting and gathering, horticultural, agrarian, and industrial (see Lenski and Lenski, 1982 for detailed discussions of these types). In each of these societies women and men share or shared a division of labor; the nature of the division is a significant factor in the relative power of the sexes (Blumberg, 1977).

The greatest sex equality existed in hunting and gathering societies, in which men were predominantly hunters and women were predominantly gatherers, but both genders performed some of each activity. These societies, which dominated for some 35,000 years, consisted of cooperative, nomadic bands of people that averaged about 40 inhabitants each. Hunting and gathering societies span all of human history; some exist even today. Population growth was nearly nonexistent in such societies, as the number of births was matched by the number of deaths. Infanticide was common because every child needed to be breastfed for several years; in addition, constant movement made it difficult to care for many children at a time.

Horticultural societies, which appeared about 9,000 years ago, were more permanent settlements. Simple horticultural societies were independent communities averaging about 100 persons each. Advanced horticultural societies consisted of somewhat larger communities and included many more communities within the society. Growing plants as the main source of food was women's invention. While women gardened, men became warriors protecting their lands. At that time the power differences between men and women began to grow. The practice of polygamy developed, in which some men had several wives. The more wives a man had for gardening, the greater the surplus of goods he could accumulate. This arrangement was the beginning of a more complex system of stratification in which some men controlled more resources than others. Some occupational specialization began to develop as well.

About 5000 to 6000 years ago, when the plow was invented and animal energy was harnessed more efficiently, fewer workers on the land could support even more people. Agrarian societies developed as settlement became increasingly permanent and social organization grew increasingly complex. Such societies were controlled by landowners, to whom the peasants paid exploitive rents for using the land. Children, especially sons, were assets because they could help to work the land and to satisfy the landlords' increasing demands. Religion became an especially powerful force; people believed that they had been created to serve the gods. This ideology was an important part of the motivation to create economic surpluses far beyond those of the past. Cities, a money exchange, and government developed. The population grew more rapidly than ever before; men worked the land and women became predominantly baby producers throughout their short life spans (Sullerot, 1971:20). Nutrition and health care were male-oriented, and female infanticide was not uncommon. Different social evaluations of women and of men were most extreme in this period and in the early stages of industrial society (Chafetz, 1984).

The accumulation of technological information in agrarian societies, the advances in transport by water, the printing press, and new developments in agriculture combined to usher in the Industrial Revolution. Lenski and Lenski (1982: 244–255) describe the revolution as having four phases. The first began in the middle of the eighteenth century and lasted about 100 years, with England as its geographic center. It was led by advances in textiles, iron, and coal. The second phase began in the middle of the nineteenth century, with the application of the steam engine to transportation. The turn of the century brought the third phase, which was marked by dramatic advances in energy technology. World War II opened the fourth phase, which was characterized by unprecedented economic growth.

The industrial revolution brought the first major step in what some people call "the liberation of women." On the one hand, industrialization provided some opportunity for gender-role change by providing women with an opportunity (though meager) to be self-supporting. On the other hand, the separation of work from the home consigned the great majority of married women to the status of housewives without function in the money economy; this development resulted in the more one-sided dependence of wives on husbands. From that time to the present, sex equality has increased slowly both within and outside the family, largely because women now have an alternative to total dependence on men.

Today we are moving quickly toward a new technological era, in which exchanging information rather than producing goods is the primary economic activity of human beings. The industrial period, which Toffler (1980) calls a *flash flood* in terms of time, centralized much of human life geographically, politically, and economically, increased cumulative knowledge, and accelerated innovation. The information society will expand the knowledge base even further, and it eliminates almost totally the need for physical prowess to participate in the economy. Thus, the labor market is open to a competition among intellectual skills possessed by both women and men.

In the late nineteenth century Tonnies (1957 [1887]) developed a typology of social organization consisting of two lifestyles, one (community) based on the unity of human beings, and the other (society) based on the separateness of human beings. In the first type, people act in response to their membership in some social group. In the second, people see themselves as separate, individual actors in society. These two concepts contrast relationships either as organic entities, whose members act as parts of the whole, or as interactions between separate and self-interested individuals who come together for specific purposes. In community, individuals remain essentially united even though separating factors are present; in society, individuals are essentially separate even though uniting activities exist (Tonnies, 1957 [1887]:64). The dominant mode affects people's thoughts and interactions with others most thoroughly.

The family is an example of community; the marketplace, an example of society. Family members share their pleasures, their sorrows, and their property; unity is based on familiarity and understanding. In the marketplace each person negotiates with others as a separate individual; interaction is a process of exchange. Individuals enter into contracts which specify a point at which two different wills intersect.

Tonnies regards these ideal typical lifestyles as representing opposing forces in human life. He distinguishes between *natural will* based on the acceptance of custom and *rational will* based on ideas about purposes and strategies. The two forces are antagonistic to each other; Tonnies describes this conflict as an important source of energy, functional in the developmental transition from agrarian to modern societies.

Tonnies is not the only scholar to describe the qualitative changes in relationships resulting from the changes of scale in human society. Durkheim (1933) wrote about *mechanical* and *organic* solidarity; Redfield (1947) discussed the *folk-urban* continuum; Bernard (1973) drew contrasts between the realms of love and/or duty and of the cash nexus. These typologies describe the process of increasing social individuation, a movement from the group to the individual as the focus of human activity.

Women's increased employment outside the home is a result of several related social forces concomitant with the developing industrial (and now postindustrial) techno-economic society. Perhaps the most important factor is the needs of economic organization. The low birthrates during the depression years of the 1930s, World War II, and the economic expansion after the war combined to create a high demand for labor in the mid-twentieth century. Most recently, the demand has called specifically for female labor because the economy has the greatest need for workers in jobs traditionally held by women, namely service and office occupations.

A second reason for the increase in women's employment outside the home is related to the dramatic change in factors affecting human reproduction. The major demographic shifts have been a decline in infant mortality, a decline in fertility, and increased life expectancy. Historically, birth and death rates were generally very similar, and there was no population growth. In agrarian societies one-half of the children did not live to the age of 14, so it was necessary to bear at least four children in the hope that two might survive to adulthood (Sullerot, 1971:62). The Industrial Revolution caused a tremendous drop in infant mortality, because of the increase in standard of living it brought, including sanitation, clean water, more adequate nutrition, and cotton clothes. Fertility also declined as children in an urban, industrial society became economic liabilities rather than assets for their parents and as more effective methods of birth control developed. It may also be that human beings are simply less fertile in densely populated urban environments because of the fast-paced and variously stressful urban lifestyle, though at this point this idea is speculation. We do know that among most species reproduction is curtailed when creatures live in densely populated environments.

The dramatic increase in life expectancy is also significant. The average life expectancy at birth for American women was 55 in 1920, 65 in 1940, 73 in 1960, and 78 in 1979 (Statistical Abstract, 1981:69). Women can expect to live well beyond their childbearing years, and because of the sex differential in life expectancy many will live several years without male partners.

All of these economic and demographic facts, as well as the fact that women now are being educated in the same proportions as men, contribute to the inevitable result that women will function increasingly in productive economic capacities. Educated women with skills to offer will want to use those skills. Barring women from economic activity would be wasteful of human resources from the viewpoint of the well-being of the whole; from an individual viewpoint, it would deny women the opportunity of self-expression and self-actualization. An additional rationale for educating and employing women is that they must be prepared to care for themselves at the end of their lives, when they may be without male partners.

The employment of women in economic production is not new; it has occurred through the ages. Only in the more affluent families could women ever be simply decorative companions to men, home managers, or specialists in motherhood. In the past, however, most of women's economic production was carried out within the home so that it could be combined with housekeeping and supervision of children. The new development is that nearly all economic production now occurs outside the home.

For the first time in human history, individuals—both women and men—can be economically independent. Families as such are no longer necessary for economic survival. This does not mean that individuals alone can be responsible for their sustenance; they depend on a wider and more complex division of labor. Yet the basis of economic interdependence and the power have moved away from families and have been centralized in larger organizations.

Women now have entered all public realms: the institutions of education, work, and politics. Gagnon and Simon (1975) point out that the fundamental axis around which social relations are organized is shifting. We have coeducation, singles bars, women in the military, and women in management, denoting a shift from homosociality to heterosociality. The shift represents a breakdown of the separate spheres of the sexes, and of course it also must affect family life. The worlds of women and men are beginning to merge; now some couples, at least, share more equally the burdens and the joys of being breadwinners, caretakers of children, and housekeepers. They are pioneers, and they do not find role sharing easy (Kimball, 1983).

Women and men in marriage partnerships traditionally have depended on each other as complements. Women depended on men as buffers against the outside world, and men on women to manage their emotional and domestic lives. This symbiosis assured males a monopoly of economic and political power (Willis, 1982:181). Now that women are giving up this pejorative sense of dependence and are seeking their share of the economic and political action, the equilibrium has been destroyed.

The institution of marriage is bound to change as society itself evolves; the roles of husband and wife change with new situations and opportunities. In the nineteenth century, the wife's place was almost exclusively at home, but her great-grand-daughter is likely to be active in several community organizations and in a paid occupation as well as in the family. This change occurred because of demographic, technological and economic advances, but it had to be accompanied by changes in the shared concept of what is feminine and what is masculine. New roles and new ideology are slowly modifying marriage, the basic man-woman union, as well.

The forces for social change have transferred many functions from the home to the marketplace, and have diminished ascriptive roles. Independence is a viable reality for each person; thus, we rely increasingly on loving and rewarding personal relationships rather than on economic functional interdependence to keep families together and functioning. This change requires human beings to be better equipped with interpersonal skills and the humanistic values necessary to make families work. The challenge for marriages today was created by the developments of societal evolution, particularly by the propensity toward social differentiation and individuation. These developments are demographic, economic, technological, and ideological. In the next sections we will elaborate on the nature of each of these changes.

POPULATION SHIFTS

Demographic changes are an important part of the complex of social and economic change that we call the Industrial Revolution. The most important demographic development associated with the new technologies was the decline in mortality. This

Table 2.1 Expected Number of Years of Life, at Birth

Year of Birth	Males	Females
1920	53.6	54.6
1930	58.1	61.6
1940	60.8	65.2
1950	65.6	71.1
1960	66.6	73.1
1970	67.1	74.7
1980	70.0	77.5
1990	71.0	78.0

Source: Table #102. Expectations of Life at Birth 1920/1983. Statistical Abstract of the U.S. (1985:69).

change led to other demographic developments: a decline in fertility and a tremendous increase in average life expectancy. In the past, high mortality had required similarly high fertility to ensure a population's survival, but now the need to produce many children has diminished dramatically.

Today a newborn female in an industrialized nation can expect to live to the age of 78, a male to the age of 71. At the beginning of the nineteenth century, life expectancy in the United States was estimated to be about 35 years (Taeuber and Taeuber, 1958). Table 2.1 shows the degree of change in expected life spans in the United States only since the early twentieth century. For females, the increase in life expectancy from 1920 to the present is nearly 24 years, for males 17.5 years. These changes result mostly from the great decline in infant and child mortality.

This decline means that women no longer have to spend as much time and energy in bearing or rearing children. In combination with the increase in life expectancy, the decline means that women can devote a smaller proportion of their lives to these activities. They have more time for other activities. Table 2.2 indicates the declines in infant mortality over the twentieth century and the concomitant decline in fertility. This decline in fertility results in smaller families; consequently, fewer women are pregnant or have small children at any one time. A smaller pro-

Table 2.2 Change in Infant Mortality and Fertility Rates

Year	Infant Mortality (per 1000 live births)	Fertility (per 1000 population)
1910	na	30.1
1920	85.8	27.7
1930	64.6	21.3
1940	47.0	19.4
1950	29.2	24.1
1960	26.0	23.7
1970	20.0	18.4
1980	12.6	15.9
1983	10.9	15.5

Source: Table #80. Live Births, Deaths, Marriages, and Divorces 1910 to 1983. Statistical Abstract of the U.S. (1985:57).

portion of women in the society are responsible for bringing up the young.

The initial fertility decline associated with the Industrial Revolution was accomplished by primitive birth control methods: abstinence, withdrawal, abortion. The trend has continued in the advanced industrialized countries even since the mid-twentieth century, with corresponding shifts in both attitudes and behavior. Birth control methods have been revolutionized, and abortion is accepted increasingly in western nations. The number of lifetime births expected by women in their twenties was close to 2.1, the minimum needed for natural population replacement, by the mid-1970s (U.S. Bureau of the Census, 1976:1). Young women may have even fewer children than predicted.

Huber (1977:341) predicts that fertility will continue to decline, and bases her prediction on the trends showing how past generations responded to the economics of child rearing. She offers an eight-point rationale: (1) the cost of raising a child continues to increase; (2) financial security for the elderly is increasingly a function of government, not of family; (3) the median levels of education for women continue to rise; (4) men increasingly desire two-earner families; (5) the need to choose between jobs and fertility persists for women; (6) maternal employment is not considered to affect children adversely; (7) the

burden and emotional expense of child rearing falls dispropor-
tionately on women; and (8) voluntary childlessness has become
respectable.

Huber (1977:343–344) believes that because of fears of economic stagnation and depopulation, governments may take
steps to make childbearing more attractive, but not too attractive; these measures will be supportive of increasing sex equality. The most feasible step is to reduce child-rearing costs for
parents, but it is unlikely that this can be done by inducing
women to stay home; thus, the time and money costs of child
rearing must be spread more widely over the age and sex structure of the population. The costs of child-care services, health-
care services, and postsecondary education may need to be
shared with nonparents in order to socialize the next generations. To be equal partners with men, women must participate
equally in the occupational system, and they can do that only to
the extent that they are not burdened differentially by child
rearing.

The revolutionary technology in controlling births is highly
significant in the changing mores between the sexes and, thus,
in the effects on marriages. The technology has been accompanied by new attitudes and values about sexual behavior. Ridley
(1972) describes how the possibility of conceiving children only
when they are wanted will have many important consequences
for women's lives. If one assumes that illegitimate births are
unwanted, illegitimacy may disappear. Premarital pregnancy,
which certainly is a factor in determining the timing of marriage,
can be reduced. Such pregnancies tend to interrupt or terminate
educational attainment for the women involved, and to have
harmful effects on their nonfamilial roles. Campbell (1970) found
that the longer a first birth is delayed, the more the wife participates in familial decision making. Birth control is a key factor in
the changing status of women within and beyond the family.

Ridley (1972:382) makes the point that the state of zero population growth itself requires that women participate more fully in
economic activities. A community with zero growth has an older
population, and although such a community is less likely to

place a premium on youth, it still must depend on the young for new ideas. In addition, it will need the ideas and the labor of both sexes to support those who are older.

In *Too Many Women?*, Guttentag and Secord (1983) explore the behavioral ramifications of another important demographic phenomenon, imbalanced sex ratios. The ratio represents the number of men per 100 women; a balanced sex ratio is 100, a higher ratio denotes more men, and a lower ratio, more women. The authors describe the *dyadic power* and the *structural power* of one sex as opposed to the other. When one sex is in short supply, relationships between the sexes potentially are affected in a similar fashion for both sexes. Members of the sex in short supply have a stronger position and are less dependent on their partners because more alternative relationships are available. This position is *dyadic power*. The individual whose sex is in short supply can negotiate more favorable outcomes within the two-person relationship; he or she is more likely to choose to leave one relationship for another, which is perceived as having a better outcome. *Structural power*, on the other hand, belongs to the sex that holds the positions of power and dominance in the institutions of society: government, business, industry, the military, science, education, and the professions. Those who hold formal power in these arenas are likely also to be influential in shaping the informal social norms of society.

Dyadic power has varied with the sex ratio at different times and places, although structural power has been in the hands of men until this time. Sex-ratio imbalances are likely to have certain effects on the behaviors of and relations between women and men. Until World War II, the ratios were generally high, with a surplus of men, but the war and the baby boom of the late 1940s and early 1950s altered the age-sex structure of society. In addition, declines in mortality and/or increases in fertility create an imbalance between numbers of men and women at the prime age for marriage because women marry men somewhat older than themselves, two and one-half years on the average. A decrease in mortality decreases the supply of potential husbands for any cohort of women because the men they marry were born in a period of higher mortality. The baby-boom years created a similar situation because the many women born at that time outnumbered the potential husbands, who were slightly older. Demographers have called this phenomenon a *marriage squeeze* (Glick et al., 1963). The low sex ratio in recent years is likely to be a causal factor in several developments: women experiencing first marriage at a later age, more women remaining single, the larger pool of divorced women at any one time, and more divorced and widowed women not remarrying.

According to Guttentag and Secord's (1983) theory, when low sex ratios prevail, the social bond of commitment in male-female relationships is weakened. The oversupply of women makes it less necessary for a man to marry to have a woman as companion and sexual partner. These circumstances, however, historically have existed in a situation in which men also held the structural power in society. Alternatively, when there are more men than women and when unattached women are scarce, they posit men's commitment to be strongest. Women gain some dyadic power at these times, which offsets men's superior structural power. Guttentag and Secord (1983:231–243) argue that these outcomes of imbalanced sex ratios may not exist in the future if men's monopoly on structural power erodes. If male-female relationships in which neither party is dominant become more common, the practice of men marrying women younger than themselves may be weakened; this change could eliminate the marriage squeeze for women born when birthrates are rising and for men born when birthrates are falling.

All these changes in social practices and structures tend to change our beliefs about the nature of women and men. The attributes that have been ascribed typically to women follow from their mother role (nurturant, domestic, soft, affectionate) or from their weak position (unassertive, submissive, passive, dependent, devious, manipulative, irrational, emotional) in work and/or marriage. The same may be said of men with respect to their more powerful positions. They have been cast as heroes, problem solvers, and rescuers because of their access to more resources and greater opportunities. With the growth of equality, gender-role identities of both sexes are likely to shift to include more of the characteristics traditionally attributed to the opposite sex.

The demographic changes that accompanied the Industrial Revolution are intertwined in a pattern of technological and economic innovation. These forces, too, have been a significant part of the social change affecting women's and men's behavior.

TECHNOLOGICAL AND ECONOMIC CHANGE

Many theorists contend that changes in social organization and relationships result from technological innovation (Huber, 1976; Ogburn, 1966; Rothschild, 1983). Technology plays a key role in defining the nature of social organization and interpersonal interaction; social norms and values are adapted to the expanded opportunities in new forms of social organization. The new behavioral norms create new attitudes and perspectives, generating interest groups and political movements. Finally, these groups and movements may bring policy and legal changes into the formal value system of the culture.

Ogburn's theory of cultural lag suggests that our ideas, beliefs, and values often lag behind actual material and organizational changes. The basic elements of social change are invention, accumulation, diffusion, and adjustment. Material inventions result from mental activity, demand, and the presence of other cultural elements. When more elements are added to the cultural base than are lost, accumulation takes place; when an invention interacts with other cultural elements, adaptation occurs. Applying this interpretation to the family, Nimkoff and Ogburn (1955) argue that technological developments altered societal organization in ways which removed essential functions from the realm of the family. In agrarian society the family was strong because it subsumed educational, economic, protective, and state functions. In the Industrial Revolution many of these functions were taken over by industries and government, leaving the family to emphasize interpersonal affection and happiness. Both production technology and reproductive technology have had important ramifications for woman's changing role and for the changing functions of the family.

Production Technology and the Changing Labor Force

Changes in the organization of production and economic activity are highly relevant to changes in American marriages. In explaining the rise of the women's movement in the late 1960s, Huber (1976) stresses that the degree of sex stratification in a society depends on the extent to which men dominate the distribution of resources outside the family. The right and the opportunity to distribute and exchange goods and services beyond the domestic unit confer prestige and power in all societies. Women have had second-class status in the job world because they bear children and consequently are expected to rear them. In order to emerge, the women's movement of the 1970s required more than the mere presence of persistent discrimination. The situation had to be perceived as unfair, and there had to be some sense that something could be done about the situation. This situation did not develop until there was a rapid increase in the employment of women, which began in World War II but became strongest after the mid-1960s. The women's movement is responsible for much of the increased awareness of sex stratification and for the change in ideology toward a more equal valuing of women and men.

Modern society is organized on an occupational basis. In agrarian society most people played the same basic roles, but today there is an extensive division of labor. People engage in specific, relatively continuous activities in order to earn a livelihood and to maintain a definite social position and status. The occupational specialization introduced by technological development places people in different positions with different perspectives on the world.

One way to describe the structure of occupations is to note the three main sectors of work in an industrialized economy. The primary sector includes activities of extracting and gathering natural resources used for food and other products (for example, mining, forestry, and agriculture). The secondary sector involves jobs that turn these raw materials into goods (producing cars, furniture, and canned food). The tertiary sector refers to all service activities, such as banking, teaching, and beauty care. Early in the industrial process most jobs are in the primary industries. In the middle stages the secondary sector is dominant; the greatest effort is devoted to producing goods. In advanced industrialization the majority of people are in service occupations. In the future the great majority of people will be in services, and most of these workers will be in information-related services. Through this changing division of labor, productive technology alters our work roles and thus affects women's and men's relative status. A high degree of sex segregation exists in the occupational structure, and women have been employed predominantly in the rising tertiary sector. In the past, men dominated the primary and secondary industries, but as these sectors decline, women and men find themselves competing more often for similar kinds of work. In sum, production technology has changed gender roles directly and indirectly through the changing nature of the labor force.

Reproductive Technology

Improvements in workplace technologies have interacted with reproductive technologies to expand the opportunities for women in the labor force. As mechanical power replaced human and animal muscle power, jobs requiring social interaction and mental skills became more plentiful, but women were only a reserve labor force as long as they could not control the frequency and timing of births.

Whicker and Kronenfeld (1986)[2] argue that change in reproductive technology (birth control) specifically can be tied most closely to change in gender roles. They point out that human societies must perform two activities for survival: produce food and essential materials for their members and reproduce themselves. They attribute women's increased labor-force participation to the collapse of the child-bearing distinction between women and men; this change, they claim, is attributable almost wholly to new birth control technology. In the past, women's lack of control over childbearing was responsible for gender-based functional specialization (Kronenfeld and Whicker, 1986:53).

In contrast, specific production technologies for home and for work have had less influence on women's role in society. New production technologies in the home have not contributed to major role changes mostly because the standards of home care have increased steadily, and for the upper and the upper middle classes the availability of domestic help has decreased steadily.

Human beings always have tried to control reproduction, beginning with various homemade vaginal barriers or solutions. Abstinence, withdrawal, extended breast feeding, and abortions have been used widely. Condoms became available in the eighteenth century to those who could afford them, but were not widely available until the late nineteenth century. At that time diaphragms and spermicides also became available. These inventions were necessary and essential in continuing the declines in fertility, which accompanied the Industrial Revolution. Finally, intrauterine devices and oral contraceptives were developed in the mid-twentieth century. More effective and more reliable birth control has helped change women's perceptions of their roles in society.

IMPLICATIONS FOR FAMILY IDEOLOGY

Changes in our material life associated with the Industrial Revolution stimulated change in our belief systems, values, and perspectives on the world. The family itself became a political issue precisely because the potential change in the relations between men and women at home and in the broader society is a matter of access to power.

American society has been the exemplary product of the classical liberal ideology, which originated with Locke and Rousseau in the seventeenth and eighteenth centuries. America's dominant ideology can be summed up in the concept of *individualism*, which includes a strong commitment to individual autonomy and independence, freedom of choice, equality of opportunity, and equality before the law. Feminism, basically an extension of this concept, calls for the same principles of classical liberalism to be applied to women as to men. Thus sex equality entails a dramatic change in the power structure of this society; and because any discussion of sex equality must include family matters, the family has emerged today as a central political issue.

The liberal democratic society of America has been experienced as truly liberal and democratic only by some people, mostly middle-class white men. If women are to enjoy the same experience, new family forms will be necessary because family stability and child rearing in recent generations have rested on prescribed gender roles that assumed different and unequal opportunities for women and for men. At the same time, human beings have genuine needs, which traditionally have been met by the role of women in the family. Women have done the essential housekeeping and child rearing; they have been a significant volunteer army in the community; they have been an underpaid and sometimes a reserve labor force in the economy. In part, the liberal society has been made more accessible to men because of the limited and restricted roles that were defined for women.

American ideology contains some inconsistency. A conflict exists between competing sets of values, neither of which is expendable: the values of caring for others and of individual creativity and productivity. Under the present social arrangements these sets of values sometimes are incompatible. On the one hand, we recognize that meaningful interpersonal relationships provide personal identity and self-worth for individuals; that these relationships thrive in stable families within a sustaining community; and that traditional "women's work"—nurturing and caring for others—is absolutely essential to our well being as individuals and as a society. On the other hand, our individualistic society stresses personal achievement. It gives highest priority to productive, creative, instrumental activities, and rewards most the activities in which men have typically engaged. Performance of expressive, integrative functions has been assured by restricting women to specific roles rather than by building a reward system that also places a high value on these endeavors.

The overall trend toward social differentiation and individuation is reaching women. As they are employed increasingly outside the home, they, too, are being liberated from ascribed roles. Yet as women begin to respond to the existing reward system, many people are recognizing the potential loss of the integrative and nurturing activities that used to enrich all of our lives. The value and the importance of this work is apparent, but we have yet to build a reward structure that assures that it will be done, now that women have the opportunity for more directly rewarded, more instrumental endeavors. If these nurturing activities are to receive their proper due, men as well as women inevitably must engage in them, and this step requires that men cultivate nurturing and expressive abilities to a greater extent than in the past.

Human beings adapt readily to changing cultural patterns, and from a sufficiently broad perspective we can see that changes in male-female relationships are taking place. Gadlin (1977), a family historian, describes the extent of adaptation specifically in the middle classes. His point is that when the ties between work and home were severed by the coming of industrialization, the developing separation of the public and the private led to a tremendous expansion of personal consciousness. Intimate relationships, as we understand them today, emerged as recently as the early decades of the nineteenth century. Intimacy in relationships accompanies individualism (Gadlin, 1977:34); both attend modernization. As a society, our awareness of the new individualism, autonomy, and independence, which was important first to men in the world of work, is far greater than our awareness of the new intimacy, human attachment, and connectedness, a domain much more central to the lives of women.

Gadlin describes family relations in four contrasting eras to show the change taking place. In colonial America personal life was not very private; households were under community authority. Households *were* businesses, schools, churches, houses of correction, and welfare institutions; interpersonal relationships were conducted within the boundaries of all these functions. The impersonal had no meaning because everything was personal in that it was carried out in a primary relationship. Peace and harmony within marriage were essential to general social stability, so emotions were considered something to be governed and controlled; thus, the formality of that period. Love and affection were not sought for their own sake, and heterosexual intimacy was fused inextricably with domination. Differences in social status, which limit the meaning of intimacy, assured that all relationships reproduced the authority structure. The equalizing potentiality of caring was contained; when women and men have very different statuses, the personal relationship has a very different meaning to each.

By the Jacksonian era of the mid-nineteenth century, the home had ceased to be the center of all social existence, and a sphere of private life emerged around the family. The change was dramatic; as Gadlin (1977:42) suggests, we might say that these circumstances created personal identity. It is only with the emergence of the personal that it becomes possible and necessary to speak of the interpersonal, specifically of intimacy. Spouses now depended on one another for a depth and range of companionship provided previously by a diversity of others. Feelings came to provide the reason for relationships, and coming together in marriage became a private rather than a public matter. Romantic love is just one sign of the expansion of personal consciousness that led to a greater interest in subjectivity. In addition, there was great concern about social cohesion; the family had lost some of its ability to sustain social order and community. The emerging sexual division of labor in the market and the home mirrored the public and the private realms.

By the Progressive Era of the early twentieth century, the economic framework of the family had fallen away, causing a

strain on the personal tie (Kennedy, 1970:39). Compulsory education, new child-rearing practices, and smaller families resulted
in more autonomous, more individuated persons. The emergence of psychology, in itself, was a sign of the development of
personal identity. More than ever before, personal identity and
interpersonal life became public matters.

The contemporary experience suggests that the meaning of
sexuality is confused, the value of intimacy subverted, and the
future of marriage uncertain. Our social relationships develop
more slowly than the economic relationships that dominate
them, but eventually they become appropriate to the conditions
in which we live.

A successful marriage encompasses rather than contradicts
personal self-fulfillment, and it requires tolerance, self-sacrifice,
and a work-at-it orientation. Even so, we need to provide greater
opportunity for the self-actualization of all people. People can
have more satisfying, passionate, loving relationships when
they are free to be equals. They must let go of needs to be
ascendant or subservient; this change requires the reshaping of
expectations in all institutions, not only marriage and the family.

NOTES

1. The term *social individuation,* as used here, refers to the idea of the individual and to the value placed on the individual which accompanies the social
differentiation of function. It represents a societal consciousness of the individual and is a very different concept from psychological individuation, a traditional
developmental term indicating the achievement of individual autonomy and
personal identity. (See the discussion of Jung under "The Relationship of Gender
to Identity," Chapter 3.)

2. See also Kronenfeld and Whicker (1986) for a similar discussion in a
shorter form.

CHAPTER THREE

Gender-Role Identity and Marriage

The explanations for the success of the dual-earner marriages explored in this book are grounded in a set of assumptions known as *identity theory*. This body of theory is embedded in turn in a wider theoretical perspective called *symbolic interaction*. In this chapter we describe this theoretical background and indicate its importance for understanding marital relationships.

CONSTRUCTING IDENTITY

Identity: The Social Self

A major premise of symbolic interaction is that the self is a product of society. Positions in structured relationships and the roles that accompany them are significant to the self. Social structure affects social behavior by shaping self-concepts, but considerable reciprocity exists; the behavior of individuals, which authenticates selves, either maintains or alters social structure.

George H. Mead (1934), the major architect of symbolic interaction theory, saw social interaction as a process from which mind, self, and society emerge together. Mind, the activity of thinking or problem solving, emerges as individuals initiate activities relating themselves to their environment. Things in the environment acquire meanings (become symbolic to individuals) through the ongoing activity of human beings; that is, objects and ideas become meaningful only when they are relevant to some problem-solving activity. People, too, acquire meaning through ongoing activity; we invest others with meanings or symbols that define them for us. Because those meanings exist, we can anticipate other people's future behavior, and we continually adjust our behavior to those anticipations. We also see ourselves as objects by attaching to ourselves symbols that emerge from interaction; those symbols are social roles, and they indicate how we are expected to behave. In short, we come to know who and what we are through interaction with others (Stryker and Serpe, 1982).

The idea of reciprocity between society and self is an important element of symbolic interaction. The expectations of social roles are sometimes ambiguous, and in most situations people have some degree of choice in the actions available to them. Positions and roles are not so discrete, however, when they are embodied in real people. Stryker and Serpe (1982:205) suggest that identity theory addresses itself to this circumstance of choice. Role identities are the answers to "Who am I?" They indicate positions in social structure that refer to discrete parts of the self. This definition assumes that we have as many role identities as we have distinct sets of structured relationships (father, friend, tennis partner, lawyer). The concept of *identity salience* assumes that each person has a salience hierarchy, which organizes role identities within the self. The hierarchy represents the relative importance of specific role identities to the individual's personality structure. An individual's *commitment* to a role identity depends on the number of persons encountered in that role and on the significance of those persons to the individual. Commitment affects identity salience, which in turn affects role-related behavior choices (Stryker and Serpe, 1982).

People constantly are faced with the necessity of locating themselves in relation to others. On the basis of certain available clues, individuals infer their own roles and those of others. When people ask "Who am I?", the answers are socially constructed roles and relationships that are actual behavior patterns identified by the participants. Those answers would be groundless if they were not ratified through interaction or doing. A person's social identity at any time is a function of validated social positions; appropriate, proper, and convincing role behavior validates one's positions for self and others.

Juhasz (1983) argues that human identity, social identity, and individual identity are all essential and mutually interdependent components of a person's overall identity. *Human identity* or human nature recognizes membership in a species. *Social identity* recognizes the pertinent categories into which the species can be sorted. *Individual identity* is a recognition of the same person despite memberships in many social categories. For Juhasz (1983:289–290) human identity or human nature is the ground from which our social identities are carved by our interactions with others. Despite enormous changes in social identities through time or space, we maintain a unique, individual sense of self throughout our lives. This is individual identity, which transcends, connects, and gives substance to our multiple and ever-changing social identities. The two elements emerge together; the capacity to occupy social roles is a prerequisite to having an individual identity, but a person must have an individual identity before he or she can occupy a social role.

The social identities that we discern as concepts and as empirical realities are anchored in human and in individual identity, and role expectations in the social structure change over the generations. Roles are derived in part from the independent performances of the many people who play them. Social identities could not exist if an enduring, all-inclusive human nature were not operating in the background. Similarly, the components of social identities could not exist in a stable society if individual, personal identities did not exist to transcend the changes in role expectations that move us from one point in time to another (Juhasz, 1983:316). These ideas are not incompatible with symbolic interaction, but rather explicate the total interdependence between society and self as well as the importance of identity as a determinant of behavior. They indicate why one must address the relationship of gender to identity to explain the changing relationships between women and men.

Gender

We can observe regularities in the differences between women's and men's behavior. Most of these differences are not necessarily determined by biological sex; sex refers to the physical structure of human beings and is determined by chromosomes, gonads, and hormones. For most people, sex is an unalterable fact, but anatomical sex does not automatically match psychological sex. The latter must develop as the person develops. We prefer the term *gender* to *sex* when referring to social-psychological processes because *gender* underlines the fact that we are speaking of learned traits or behaviors. Gender refers to clusters of culturally constructed characteristics regarded as appropriate for males or females in a specific society; these clusters are called *femininity* and *masculinity* (Gould and Kern-Daniels, 1977; Unger, 1979). Sex is innate or ascribed; gender is learned or achieved. For the purposes of this discussion, we will distinguish and use three interrelated terms: gender identity, gender role, and gender-role identity.

Gender Identity

Psychologists traditionally have considered gender identity as one's sense of self as male or female. This is a very deep sense, which may even be unconscious (La Torre, 1979:7), and it is the core around which a definition of the self and personality is formed. Psychologists assume that a clear sense of physical maleness or femaleness is essential to psychological health because of the fundamental differences in sexual functioning between adult males and females; once this sense has been established, it is relatively resistant to change. This early labeling of physical sex is important to a child's psychological development because it begins the sex-typing process through which the child acquires the characteristics considered appropriate for his or her sex in a particular culture. The constellations of personality traits, attitudes, preferences, and behaviors referred to as masculinity and femininity are the gender roles that a person learns through the sex-typing process.

Gender Role

All human groups are composed of people who occupy various positions or ranks within the group. Every position carries a set of prescribed behaviors (norms) that together make up a role or a blueprint to indicate how a person should act. Some sociologists (e.g., Lorber, 1987; Stacy and Thorne, 1985) regard gender as a system of relational social statuses embedded in the social order. Like class or race, gender is ever-present across all social networks, a ubiquitous part of the social structure that one cannot escape. We are concerned here with the degree to which gender-role prescriptions are incorporated into individuals' self-concepts. Gender is a pervasive part of the structure of social life because gender roles are societal roles rather than referring to some more limited social group. Societal gender roles have a strong influence on more specific roles within less inclusive groups, such as families, which are typically (if not always) fulfilled by women or by men, such as the wife or husband roles.

Doyle (1985:88–90), in fact, specifies normative societal gender-role expectations for women and for men, and for women he includes other expectations as well, such as being a mother or a wife. He calls these expectations *the motherhood mandate* and *the marriage mandate.* For most of our history, much of a woman's early socialization experience has indicated that having a baby and becoming a mother are the central feature of a woman's life and the very core of her identity as a person. Motherhood is not only prescribed for females; it is her raison d'etre. Second to the motherhood mandate in importance is the marriage mandate. For many women marriage was and still is a rite of passage into the world of adults. With marriage, women take on the primary responsibility of being a homemaker. Other expectations also exist for women, such as providing beauty, graciousness, and tenderness to social circumstances; these are equally pervasive but somewhat less central to the female gender role.

Normative gender-role expectations for males do not focus on parenting and marriage as strongly as those for females. Instead men are supposed to exhibit a loose-knit set of prescriptive themes. Doyle (1985:90) suggests five[1] normative expectations: (1) the antifeminine element: men must be opposite to women to be manly; (2) the successful element: men must surpass others at work, sports, or whatever they do; (3) the aggressive element: men are enjoined to fight for what they consider right; (4) the sexual element: men must live up to the norm of male as sexual initiator or controller; and (5) the self-reliant element: men must be cool, unflappable, in control, and tough in most situations.

Broverman et al. (1970), among others, have documented the consensual beliefs in society about the differences between men and women. In general, men are expected to be independent, aggressive, objective, dominant, rational, adventurous, strong, decisive, and physical; as indicated above, they are to exhibit the opposite of the alleged feminine characteristics. Women, on the other hand, are expected to be sensitive, emotional, gentle, expressive, quiet, warm, nurturing, intuitive, sensual, and pleasing to behold. Not all males or all females fulfill the norms prescribed for them, as described by Doyle or as indicated by the stereotyped trait clusters, but that fact does not deny the presence of the norms. When men exhibit a high level of masculine characteristics and women a high level of feminine characteristics, with the relative exclusion of the opposite type of characteristic, they are regarded as sex-typed.

Gender-Role Identity

While gender role refers to society's prescriptions for masculine or feminine qualities for males and females respectively, gender-role identity refers to the degree to which an individual internalizes those societal prescriptions. Thus, gender-role identity, as far as it can be identified, is likely to be a more specific and more significant predictor of behavior than biological sex. In this book gender-role identity refers explicitly to the degree to which people incorporate traditional masculine or feminine role definitions into their own self-concepts. This term differentiates the internalizing of society's gender-role definitions from the basic sense of maleness or femaleness noted above as gender identity. As children establish a gender identity, they begin to notice that some behaviors are encouraged and some are discouraged for males or for females. Through the socialization process known as sex-typing, individuals acquire and develop some pattern and level of masculine or feminine characteristics and incorporate them into their own sense of self. This aspect of individual identity is one's gender-role identity.

Several writers offer qualitative descriptions of masculinity and femininity that seem to suggest a deeper, more psychological difference in the approach to life exhibited typically by the two sexes. Simone de Beauvoir (1953), for example, describes men as *transcendent* and women as *immanent*. She considers transcendence to refer to autonomy and self-determination, the ability to excel and to go beyond limits. Immanence, in contrast, suggests being static or limited, living near others. De Beauvoir believed that people attain liberty and meaning in life through their exploits and projects; they act on the world, which leads to transcending their immediate situation. While men may act on and move beyond their present state (transcendence), women typically remain in immanence, a situation of restriction and confinement that they rarely transcend.

Gutmann (1965) describes masculine and feminine ego styles respectively as *allocentric* and *autocentric*. The allocentric ego tends to experience its own separateness from others and to objectify others. The autocentric ego has more permeable boundaries; distinctions between self and other and between oneself and one's environment simply are more blurred. Gutmann conducted some empirical tests and found, for instance, that male college students wrote about themselves and others in objective, individualistic, distant ways. Female students described their experiences in relatively subjective, interpersonal, immediate ways.

The more generalized concepts of *agency* and *communion* offered by Bakan (1966) are defined in a way that allows an individual to have both qualities. Bakan says that these are the two fundamental modalities in the existence of all living forms. *Agency* refers to the existence of an organism as an individual being, and *communion* to the individual's participation within a larger organism of which it is a part. Agency is manifest in isolation, alienation, aloneness, and the urge to master. Communion is manifest in contact, openness, union, and noncontractual cooperation. Men have been expected to specialize in agency, women in communion.

Perhaps the best-known qualitative comparison is Parsons's and Bales's (1953) contrast between the *instrumental* and the *expressive* dimensions of socialization. This description is more sociological than psychological in that Parsons and Bales are describing people's roles in interpersonal interaction and discussing how those roles are functional necessities for all groups. They assume, however, that women have the skills and the propensity to adopt the expressive orientation and that men are inclined toward the instrumental orientation; they see this specialization exemplified especially in the family. Action is instrumental if it involves orientation to goals outside the immediate relational system; it is expressive if it focuses on the relations among individuals within a social group. The rewards for instrumental action tend to be more extensive or more impersonal (power, status, material resources), while the rewards for expressive action are interpersonal (intrinsic, more emotionally direct, more immediately reciprocal).

The pairs of contrasting concepts described by these authors have been used to describe masculine and feminine tendencies. It is apparent that both elements in each pair are important and essential for human life, but the dichotomies suggest how men and women have incorporated one element or the other more deeply into their personalities through socialization. Often they become instrumental or expressive specialists. Gender identity provides the very core of the self, but gender-role identity—the personality characteristics that one acquires as life proceeds and the social roles that become significant to one's self-concept—also are highly significant. Although these personality components tend to be malleable, they shape the individual's wants and needs, what he or she will value and find comfortable in life experiences and in human relationships, and how he or she will behave in specific circumstances.

The Relationship of Gender to Identity

Lillian Rubin's (1983) provocative explanation for difficulties in intimate relationships between the sexes originates with the relationship between developing gender identity and developing the individual self. Every child must develop an independent, coherent, and continuing sense of self separate from his or her early caretaker. Both the physical self and the psychological self are important to one's sense of who he or she is, and the development of self occurs through a separation process. Two parts of the process (Rubin, 1983:54) are the crystallization of a gender identity and the maintenance of ego boundaries, boundaries of the self that serve to set us off from the rest of the world. This separation process necessarily is different for girls and for boys, says Rubin, because a woman mothered them both. Developing gender identity is more difficult for a boy because of the differences between mother and son. Developing ego boundaries is more difficult for a girl because of the daughter's close identification with the mother.

"When a boy raised by a woman confronts the need to establish his gender identity, it means a profound upheaval in his internal world" (Rubin, 1983:55). His attachment and identification with his mother as main caregiver are primary, but in order to identify with his maleness, he must renounce the connection with this person who seems a part of himself. Because he must repress this identification, his attachment to his mother becomes ambivalent. He needs her, but he can no longer be certain that she will be there. To protect against this pain he builds a set of defenses against the needs, wishes, and feelings associated with the relationship. He develops ego boundaries that are fixed and firm, and that separate him rigidly from others.

Because there are no obvious differences between a girl and her mother, the process of establishing a gender identity is much easier for girls than for boys, but the problem of separating—of defining and experiencing self as an autonomous, bounded individual—is more difficult (Rubin, 1983:58). The girl does not need to displace the internalized representation of the loved mother. Consequently, she has no need to build defenses against attachment, and therefore no need to build rigid boundaries. Thus a woman's ego boundaries are more permeable. In describing the acquisition of gender identity and the development of self, Rubin suggests how this process probably increases the propensity for males and females to adopt the qualitative dimensions associated with their sex, as described earlier. To some extent, these differences also may be attributable to having female caretakers.

The consideration of gender-role identity, however, involves a different level of analysis: the focus is on here-and-now social interaction. Although some propensities develop early in life, the characteristics described as typically masculine or feminine also are normative behaviors and attitudes, and are reinforced continually through social interaction with significant others. Many of these characteristics are associated closely with specific roles in society that are also sex-typed, such being mothers or fathers, nurses or doctors, flutists or tuba players, gymnasts or boxers. The role expectations that exist in the social environment are strong determinants of one's behavior in a specific circumstance; if an individual finds performance of that role especially comfortable and fulfilling, the associated characteristics will become a part of that person's identity and sense of self.

Symbolic interaction theorists assume that social interaction is fluid and changing precisely because people vary to some extent in their role performances. Consequently, both social structure and selves are fluid and changing. Although in significant ways we are the same person at age 40 as at age 20, we are also very different. We have had experiences and interactions that affect our role performances and our identities; we grow and change. Some researchers (Abrahams et al., 1978; Feldman et al., 1981) have shown that adult men and women modify their gender-role identities and gender-role attitudes as a function of the life situations in which they find themselves. Stage of family life was shown to be important for gender-related self-attributions and for attitudes toward traditional or more egalitarian gender-role norms. People are variously able to meet changing expectations in their social environments, depending on what roles and personality characteristics are most important and most central to their self-concepts.

Joseph Pleck's (1981) analysis of the male gender role concludes that psychologists may have created a fiction with respect to masculinity (and implicitly, femininity). He suggests (1981:4) that psychologists posit an innate psychological need to develop a gender-role identity. They assume that human beings are programmed to learn a traditional gender role as part of normal psychological development. From this point of view, culturally defined gender roles do not restrict an individual's potential, but provide a necessary external structure without which individuals could not develop normally. This view suggests that the problem is not the nature of the traditional roles but that so many people fail to fit them.

Pleck believes that for much of the twentieth century the psychologists' paradigm describing the male gender role gave intellectual shape and scientific legitimacy to all men's deep-seated cultural concerns about masculinity. The early 1970s, however, saw a growing dissatisfaction with the traditional methods of conceptualizing sex differences and gender-role identity. The concept of androgyny, not a new idea, was rediscovered (Heilbrun, 1973). This term has been used in literature and psychology to represent a blending of the masculine and feminine characteristics in life, and a kind of personal wholeness. Pleck believes that androgyny is an important transitional concept to a whole new way of viewing gender roles, which has emerged both in the social sciences and in the wider society. Instead of seeing traditional gender roles as desirable and regarding their internalization via the development of gender-role identity as the goal of psychological development, the new interpretation emphasizes the possibility of androgyny and views the special-ized roles as limiting and constricting. Pleck calls the new inter-pretation of gender roles the sex role strain paradigm. Whereas the old paradigm assumed an innate psychological need for sex-typed traits, the central arguments of the new paradigm stress sex-typed traits as responses for obtaining social approval and for situational adaptation.

This new paradigm finds the source of gender-role problems in the lack of fit between gender-role stereotypes and reality in the social environment, not in the lack of fit between individuals and gender-role stereotypes. The "situational adaptation" argu-ment, which is important in the transition to the new paradigm, implies that particular personality characteristics, whether sex-typed or androgynous, lead to good or bad psychological adjust-ment only in the context of particular situations. There is no evidence for an intrinsic relationship between sex typing and global measures of adjustment (Lenney, 1979). Both men and women are required increasingly to function in situations calling for both masculine and feminine skills. On the other hand, many individuals still function in environments requiring only traditional sex-typed skills. The relationship between sex-typing and adjustment does not result from some inherent psychologi-cal relationship, but depends on the specific situational de-mands of external environments.

The new paradigm describing strain is much more consistent than other paradigms with an interactionist view of personality. Traditional psychological theories view personal traits as resid-ing within the individual in a more or less enduring fashion, while an interactionist view suggests that identities may be more situational or more strongly associated with the roles one plays. Locksley and Colten (1979) contend that the content of gender roles may be reified personality characteristics associated with adult social roles. Hiller and Philliber (1985) found a significant relationship between the assertiveness component of gender-role identity and sex type of occupation and between assertiveness and extent of education among women. In addition we found a significant relationship between the sensitivity component of gender-role identity and the performance of housework among men. Does gender exist predominantly in the social structure or in the person?

Because the answer is probably "both," this may not be the important question. The force of expectations in the environment is vitally important to the determination of gender-role identity; people can and do change to some extent in a lifetime, as well as across generations. Obviously, however, not all people change, or change readily; individuals appear to vary greatly. People face a variety of circumstances and bring a variety of histories to the moment. It is our contention that those who are able to behave more flexibly and who have the resources apparent in both masculine and feminine trait clusters will be more successful in modern marriages, whether because they are more capable of change or because their social circumstances make different demands. This quality has been identified as psychological androgyny, and a great deal of research is being conducted regarding its causes and consequences.

Some time ago Carl Jung called attention to the need for all individuals to recognize and integrate within themselves those traits in the culture usually associated with the opposite sex. He believed that this integration was essential to personal wholeness and maturity. Jung called the process of growth *individuation* and considered it a lifelong journey (see Olds, 1981; Singer, 1973). Particularly since the early 1970s, theorists have stressed that human beings need to cope with the demands of life represented by both the instrumental and the expressive dimensions of action. Maslow's early work (1970; 1971) on self-actualization suggests that androgyny leads to a more fully human life. Later work by Bem (1974; 1975) emphasizes this view; Bem provided the first method of measuring masculinity and femininity in a manner that allowed androgyny to be seen as a third variation of gender-role identity.

In her comprehensive review of androgyny research, Cook (1985) depicts what androgyny is and is not, and describes in detail the evolution of recent research. She notes carefully (1985:19–20) that androgyny is not synonymous with economic or sexual emancipation and is not a goal of the women's liberation movement; it is not the absence of gender-role differentiation of inconsequential sex differences; it is not physical hermaphroditism or bisexuality. Cook says that androgyny is simply the simultaneous possession of masculine and feminine characteristics by a given person. As a theoretical approach in psychology, it recognizes masculinity and femininity as independent psychological domains, desirable for both sexes.

In general, people tend to label the complementary clusters of positive masculine and feminine traits as mutually exclusive and as more desirable for one sex than for the other, and sex-typed individuals have internalized society's sex-appropriate standards for desirable behavior. Bem (1974) saw some negative outcomes in this sex-typing process: individuals were prevented from engaging in adaptive behavior that was not sex-typical. She found deviants who exhibited these characteristics in a more balanced fashion to be healthier (1975). Bem's more recent research has shifted to a focus on cognitive processing (1981a; 1981b). Individuals differ, she believes, in the extent to which they apply culturally based criteria to appropriate behavior for women and for men. In this later work, Bem is concerned less with the content of masculinity and femininity and more with whether an individual classifies perceptions readily into the two classes and acts upon them. She differentiates individuals by whether or not their self-concepts and their behaviors are organized on the basis of gender (1981a: 356).

In sum, Pleck (1981:92–93) considers androgyny to be a transitional concept, rooted in the old paradigm emphasizing the importance of masculinity (and femininity) but pointing toward the new paradigm, which emphasizes the strain generated by gender roles. Bem's studies suggest that the mechanism underlying the relationship between sex typing and adjustment is situational adaptation. The analysis presented here is rooted in these perspectives. In the attempt to understand how gender-role identity may affect and be affected by the intimate marital relationship, we are particularly interested in the situational adaptation of partners in dual-earner marriages. Androgyny may be more functional than the earlier paradigm for this new type of marital relationship.

IDENTITY IN COMPATIBLE MARRIAGES

Playing roles and being oneself represent human behavior respectively at the social and the individual level of analysis. Human beings naturally do both, and both behaviors are important so that human societies can live, grow, and change together. To the extent that we play roles, we function to meet the needs of the social system in which we live; we can see our behavior as determined predominantly by the expectations of those around us and by the social structure in which we live. This aspect of human behavior provides social life with the necessary order and stability. To the extent that we behave as individuals and consistently express our own uniqueness, we are taking initiative and being creative. This aspect of human behavior provides some of the potential for change and growth in our lives and in society.

Much of our discussion suggests that some of the present-day marital difficulty is because of people's attachment to social roles and to their unwillingness or inability to deviate from these roles. Exacerbating this difficulty, present social circumstances demand that women and men let go of some traditional roles; those circumstances demand more individuality and flexibility. Roles are not bad; all societies and groups require them in order to survive. Every society has included some gender-role distinctions, which have functioned to help sustain that society. Social systems inevitably require their members to take certain roles; unless they do so, those systems cannot produce the results for which they have been organized. This principle applies to systems as simple as a marriage or as complex as the world economy, in which each nation plays a role. When a person performs roles suitably, he or she is regarded as normal; that individual does not behave in a deviant fashion, and order is maintained.

Any group must allow some room for variation in role performances. In this way norms and, hence, social structures change and adapt. Role relationships and interpersonal relationships differ greatly. Roles are inescapable. If they are not played, the social system will not work. A role is a repertoire of behavior patterns that must be followed in appropriate contexts; ideally, behavior irrelevant to the role is suppressed. Yet it is always a person who plays the role, and this person is a self. All too often the roles people play do not do justice to the entirety of their selves; they may have no opportunity just to be themselves. In fact, these persons may be immersed so deeply in roles that they do not even know their own selves. By contrast, human beings interact as whole selves in interpersonal relationships. They expose who they are (their beliefs, values, feelings) at deeper and deeper levels. Marriage involves roles, but it is also potentially the most intimate of all interpersonal relationships.

Jourard (1971) discusses how, in our culture, women and men are trained so thoroughly to be instrumental leaders and expressive caretakers respectively, that they are often oblivious to situations that demand the opposite kind of interaction. He says men trained by their upbringing to assume the instrumental role tend more than women to relate to other people on an "I-it" basis; they are more adept than women at relating to others impersonally. Men are more likely to see people as the embodiment of roles rather than as persons enacting roles, and typically do not take things as personally as women. Studies of leadership show that the most effective leaders of groups maintain an optimum distance from their followers, thereby avoiding the distraction of overintimate, personal knowledge of the followers' immediate feelings and needs. Women are more likely to find it difficult to keep their interpersonal relationships impersonal; they sense and respond to other person's feelings even in a supposedly official transaction. According to Jourard (1971:36–37), women also respond more readily to their own feelings toward the other person, sometimes appearing to forget the original purpose of the impersonal transaction.

Hennig and Jardim (1977), too, have studied women's behavior in the workplace. They point out that women often must be able to focus on the task at hand regardless of individual feelings; their findings suggest women who are successful in the occupational world generally emphasize a task orientation above a concern for interpersonal relationships. When women continue to emphasize interpersonal relationships in their work at the expense of a task orientation, they often find themselves passed over for promotion at the upper levels.

Of course both women and men also need some insight and empathy in their impersonal lives, and certainly they must have it in their personal lives. We know a great deal about motivating and training for instrumental achievements, but much less about promoting the expressive skills. Because women are trained to be comforters, they engage in and receive more self-disclosure than men; they are more transparent (Jourard, 1971:37). Perhaps engaging in considerable spontaneous self-disclosure is the mechanism that promotes insight and empathy among women. If so, we should encourage men to disclose themselves spontaneously more often. Being in touch with one's personal identity and sharing one's uniqueness openly and freely with an intimate partner is essential to a truly successful egalitarian marriage.

Intimacy and Growth in Relationships

Identity, intimacy, marriage, and growth are tied together inextricably in the life process. One must recognize a unique personal identity before one can share it: that is, before one can be intimate with another. One also needs intimate relationships to know oneself; they provide daily confrontation with another person, which repeatedly defines our boundaries for us. Marriage and friendships provide such relationships. The marital relationship is potentially the closest and most fulfilling of human relationships in which people can maximize their own growth.

Each day we are confronted with choices about how much of ourselves to reveal to others; should we permit another to know us for ourselves or should we camouflage what is real to sustain an image or a peaceful relationship, to protect others from hurt or ourselves from rejection? Jourard (1971:vii) says that this protection is costly because when we hide ourselves successfully from others, we also lose touch with our real selves. When people can disclose themselves completely to others, they learn how to increase their contact with their real selves and may be more able to direct their lives. Self-disclosure flows from an attitude of love and trust; we strive to know those we love and we let them know us, thereby permitting them to love us totally.

We expect people to disclose and to be transparent in families, but there is a great deal of evidence to show that this is not the case. Children do not know parents; parents do not know what their children think or do; husbands and wives often are strangers (Jourard, 1971:6). A major function of love relationships with family members and friends is to have one's self-concept validated by receiving the understanding and support of other human beings. If a person keeps his self hidden, it cannot be validated.

Intimacy is sharing freely one's innermost thoughts and feelings with another, but intimacy has not always existed in marriage at the levels that we recognize today. There is a new emphasis on intimacy and personal disclosure, perhaps especially in the last two decades. Safilios-Rothschild (1981), writing about the change that occurred in the 1970s, says that men react negatively to the disclosure of women's strengths and withdraw from their protective role, consequently making the women feel insecure and rejected. Women, on the other hand, react negatively to men's disclosure of weaknesses. They are frightened or disappointed, and withdraw their admiration and attachment; consequently men wish to escape from the tyranny of commitment and responsibility. Neither women nor men have learned yet that both men and women have strengths and weaknesses.

Both sexes need togetherness and self-disclosure as well as aloneness and silence. Both need commitment and continuity with others as well as some time for freedom and escape for themselves.

Robert Seidenberg (1973:30) says that marriage offers the major opportunity in life for personal growth. Genuine growth comes only with frustrations and satisfactions, in which learning and doing are involved inextricably. Although these growth processes might be experienced elsewhere, only in marriage is one likely to confront oneself day in and day out through another being. It is this unavoidable confrontation that makes the difference. Connected closely with the quest for identity is conjugal living, with its life- and growth-promoting force. The need for affinity, being and doing with another, brings mature fulfillment and ultimately ensures the stability of identity.

Each individual can originate action that changes the world for himself or herself and for others. A person embodies projects—plans, inventions, creations—that will be disclosed in time to the world. Projects can be seen as vows or commitments to transform oneself and the world in some way. First they are imagined; then, when consummated, they become perceptible to others. If we love ourselves, we love our projects; they are our lives. When we love someone else we also love their projects, and we act to facilitate them. If spouses love one another they confirm their partners in their projects by helping them, even if the help takes the form of leaving the partner alone. People who love each other treasure their own and each other's freedom, but also wish to meet each other's needs. When conflicts of interest arise, one person must submit to the other, but in a loving relationship this is not always the same person.

Growth involves achieving some balance between (on one hand) taking control and acting as an individual and (on the other) letting go and submitting to the spontaneous flow of events. Wisdom is knowing when to act in which manner, and being in touch with one's individual self can facilitate these decisions. Some individuals are more intent than others on maintaining or striving for a certain self. Typically they are bound more strongly by expectations, either their own or those of others. Others live more in the present, more spontaneously. Forisha (1978) calls the former type of people *role-oriented* and the latter type *process-oriented*.

Role-oriented individuals are more likely to prefer ordering their lives in a set, predictable fashion. They may direct energy toward maintaining some self that existed in the past or toward constructing some possible future self rather than toward living simply in the present. Such a person may be less likely to give up attachment to traditional gender roles, which represent stability and provide guidelines and structure. Process-oriented individuals are more in touch with their feelings of the moment and are more likely to accept themselves and others as they are. Because they can live with or without the approval of certain others, they can afford to be more open (Forisha, 1978:88).

Regardless of the degree to which we are role-oriented, everyone must come to terms with the traditional masculine and feminine forms in society. These forms affect us throughout life and are evident in our thinking, our feeling, and our sense of identity. The forms provide some sense of security for individuals who lack inner strength; many women are happy to be protected and cared for financially, even though the price may be accepting an implicit evaluation of themselves as less competent and less capable. Even those who prefer to give up the dependent role find themselves slipping back into it gratefully on occasion. Men, too, derive a sense of power and attractiveness from the traditional masculine script. Although usually they take for granted their efforts to achieve, they become aware of the power they derive from their assumed instrumental superiority when they fear that their achievement is being surpassed by that of a woman (Forisha, 1978:172–180).

We follow the old role scripts partly because we want to be attractive to the opposite sex, particularly our marriage partners or partners-to-be. In the search for security and stability, we often emphasize roles at the expense of spontaneity; that emphasis may hinder our personal development as well as our partners'. In such a relationship, love is a cover for power when we sacrifice our needs for our partners' needs and expect the same in return. By withholding the truth from the other person, we remove his or her power of decision; this is a method of control. If roles define relationships, both power and love are limited, and one becomes confused with the other. If partners are more process-oriented, however, both can be powerful and loving. Each can focus on the other person's wants, needs, and capabilities rather than conforming to what they "ought" to do.

Individual Identity and Marital Stability

The traditional gender-role definitions and modes of relating in marriage serve more to maintain the status quo than to foster growth. Jourard (1971:103) hypothesizes that conformity to familial roles can produce dispiriting, stressful, untenable situations, which culminate in physical illness for some people and in neurotic or psychotic breakdown for others.

In the United States, objective reasons for enforcing conformity are vanishing. The forms of family life that were relevant in rural and earlier urban life and that helped to produce the industrial complex have become obsolete (Jourard 1971:106). Most Americans are released from circumstances of dire economic necessity. To experiment more creatively with forms of marriage, family life, schooling, and leisure pursuits requires such freedom. Yet to live more spontaneously and more existentially is threatening to most of us; it requires personal security, faith, and trust.

It is a challenge to worry less about conforming consistently to gender-role prescriptions and simply to be oneself at the moment. Some, if not most, androgynous individuals may experience greater anxiety and stress at times than more traditionally sex-typed individuals. Two possible explanations are (1) that they are confronting and sometimes disregarding social norms, and (2) that they experience their inner conflicts more deeply than do other individuals. In general, we do not always look kindly on those who choose their own way. Androgynous people also are likely to be more aware of themselves and others; they know what is going on both inside and outside themselves. Consequently, they may respond more authentically to the pain of the human condition, although they also may experience a more profound satisfaction and delight in living than others (Forisha, 1978:101).

The ego ideal of men is generally a confluence of breadwinner, husband, parent, and achiever; these roles are more or less compatible. For a woman, on the other hand, the ego ideal of achiever may clash sharply with her ideal perceptions of womanhood. She cannot be a "good" wife, mother, and homemaker and aspire readily at the same time to "soul-satisfying" individual goals. The task of integrating the two roles is difficult because she is made to feel guilty if other aspirations impinge on her role as a mother. Consequently the woman needs help not only from an exceptional mate, who genuinely understands her struggle and provides a proper milieu and opportunity for her fulfillment, but also from structures in the wider society (Seidenberg, 1973:160).

All roles, including gender roles, become less ascribed with modernization. Psychologically, women and men are likely to become less dependent on stereotyped gender roles in defining themselves. They are likely to become more individualistic, and because of an increased awareness of their individual uniqueness, they should have a greater capacity for intimacy. The more intimacy couples can achieve, the more likely they will be to have satisfying, stable marriages.

NOTE

1. Four of these themes (all but the sexual element) were described originally by Brannon (1976).

CHAPTER FOUR

The Distribution of Perceived Marital Quality

In recent years the economic, replacement, and socialization functions of the family have declined in importance. Before women had the opportunity for paid employment they depended on men to provide sufficient resources for their livelihood. This economic bond made women captives in their own marriages. They were fortunate if their marriages were good, but they had no viable options if they were not. The wages from available menial labor would not provide sufficient income to sustain a comparable lifestyle. The opening of the labor force to women has increased the earning power of all women. Although an employed woman would lose the economic advantages of pooled resources if she chose to separate from her husband, she can earn enough to support herself sufficiently well so that separation becomes an alternative in an unsatisfying relationship.

The importance of the family in childbearing and child rearing also has declined in recent years. Women have fewer children than in the past and concentrate their childbearing within relatively few years. Effective means of contraception, declining infant mortality, and the reduced need for child labor have contributed to a reduction in the importance of bearing children. In addition, the stigma of childbirth outside marriage has diminished somewhat, making it acceptable for women without husbands to bear children.

Alternatives to the family have developed to provide for the socialization of children. By the age of six all children leave the home for most of the day to attend school, where they are taught many of the skills they will need as adults. Younger children may spend their days in child-care facilities or with an adult who is paid to look after them. Although the effects of these arrangements are still debated, it is clear that many children who spend few daytime hours with their parents grow up to become functioning adults.

While the economic, replacement, and socialization functions of the family have declined, the need for the family to provide emotional support to its members has increased. Many adults' occupational roles are not highly gratifying; much of the work is routine and becomes boring after a few years. By the time many workers have been in the labor force for 10 to 15 years it becomes evident that they will not achieve the goals they set for themselves. They will be forced to spend most of their lives in positions which are less than they desired, doing work that they find uninteresting. Those who are fortunate enough to hold gratifying jobs frequently find themselves in positions of high stress. They may be administrators or professionals who are responsible for making decisions or producing solutions to problems, and their decisions often have consequences for others. The work is gratifying because of the challenge, but the costliness of mistakes raises the stress level.

Most of the roles that adults perform, including occupational roles, are limited and defined; one is expected to perform one's role without complications. Associates are not expected to be interested in an individual's personal problems or needs, and a supervisor who knows that an individual has problems may decide against giving that person new opportunities. Colleagues may use knowledge of weaknesses to gain advantage in competitive situations; others in exchange relationships can exploit weaknesses to their advantage. In general, individuals protect themselves by limiting their interactions to task activities relevant to the roles they are performing. Impression management is a constant concern; the need to maintain a positive presentation of self makes it difficult to receive emotional support.

Family relationships ideally provide the individual with greater opportunity to receive emotional gratification. Couples typically are drawn together for romantic, not instrumental reasons. In the decision to marry, a person seldom considers the prospective spouse's ability to cook a good meal, keep a clean house, or earn a good income. Instead, character is the focus of attention. Being a good person (however that is defined) is more important than being good at some set of tasks. Finding acceptance and support from the other person, although that person knows one's inadequacies, becomes critical to a stable marriage.

In short, the stability of marriages in contemporary society depends on the quality of the interaction between spouses. In today's marriages husbands and wives are not bound to each other by strong exchange relationships; each is capable of providing or securing basic goods and services without the other. The important element is emotional gratification, and emotional gratification depends on the quality of the interaction.

THE WORK AND FAMILY STUDY

The Work and Family Study was designed to study factors related to marital quality in contemporary society. Between October 1982 and March 1983, we conducted 489 interviews with husbands and wives married to each other. We selected couples by randomly dialing households in the Cincinnati, Ohio metropolitan area. Because we were especially interested in couples in which both spouses were employed in the labor force, those couples are overrepresented in the sample. We made appointments with couples who agreed to be interviewed; two team members, one man and one woman, went to the couple's home to interview the husband and the wife respectively at the same time in separate rooms. The interviews took about one-half hour to complete. (Details of the sample can be found in the Appendix.)

Couples who participated in the Work and Family Study were asked what they had looked for in a spouse before they married. In keeping with our belief that people marry for emotional reasons, only 8% of the husbands and 11% of the wives said that they had looked for someone to fill traditional roles such as provider or housekeeper. Furthermore, few men (12%) and fewer women (7%) had sought a physically attractive person. Almost everyone had looked for someone with whom they felt compatible, a good, kind, or stable person for whom they felt love. Among husbands and wives alike, about 20% felt that the most important thing was to find someone they loved. Another 15% emphasized the importance of a spouse's morality and a similar number had looked for stability.

Husbands and wives differed, however, on the importance of both compatibility and kindness. One-quarter of the husbands but only about one-tenth of the wives stated that compatibility was an important criterion in their search for a spouse. Wives were more concerned than husbands about their spouses' kindness (17% compared to 4%). It is impossible to know exactly what husbands had in mind when they mentioned compatibility, but the fact that wives frequently mentioned kindness suggests that husbands are expected to be sensitive and to meet their wives' emotional needs. A man's ability to provide for a family's material well-being may or may not be a necessary condition to attract a wife today, but for many women it is an insufficient condition.

To assess marital quality as perceived by husbands and wives, we asked participants a series of questions about the frequency of events in their marriages. The questions were adapted from an earlier study conducted by Graham Spanier (1976). Four of the events suggested a negative marital experience: quarreling, getting on each other's nerves, regretting marrying, and striking physically. The other four were positive: planning for the future, confiding in each other, feeling satisfied, and spending leisure time together. Positive and negative events were alternated in the interview, and participants were asked whether each event occurred all of the time, most of the time, some of the time, hardly ever, or never. The distribution of responses for husbands and for wives is shown in Table 4.1.

Although almost everyone reported negative events in their marriages, few reported that those experiences were frequent. Nobody said that they quarreled, had regrets about marrying, or were struck by their spouses all of the time; few respondents said that these events or that spouses getting on their nerves, occurred even most of the time. The great majorities of husbands and of wives reported that they never regretted marrying their spouses and never were struck by them. Marriages in which the participants perceive frequent quarrels, frequently get on each other's nerves, frequently regret marrying, or frequently are struck by their marital partners are obviously in deep trouble. People in such marriages may be unable to ignore their problems; either they reduce the tension to a manageable level or they separate from their partners.

Negative events were perceived by participants in the study as occurring only some of the time or less often. Over 90% of both husbands and wives said that they quarreled or had a spouse who got on their nerves either some of the time or hardly ever. More than 85% hardly ever or never were hit by their spouses or regretted marrying them; the majority reported that these things never happened. It is interesting to observe that almost twice as many husbands (25%) as wives (13%) reported being struck by their spouses.

Although few people reported frequent negative events in their marriages, it does not follow that positive events occurred. Approximately one-third of husbands and wives alike reported that they planned for the future or spent leisure time together only some of the time or less; one-fourth did not confide in their spouses more often than some of the time. Over 90%, however, felt satisfied with their marriages all or most of the time.

We created a summary measure of marital quality by combining the responses to the eight items. For each item we assigned a score of 0 to the response indicating the most negative marital quality and a score of 4 to the response indicating the most positive quality. The scale had a possible range from 0 to 32; the

Table 4.1 Distribution of Quality of Marriage in the Work and Family Survey (N=489), in Percentages

Question	All the Time	Most of the Time	Some of the Time	Hardly Ever	Never
Husbands:					
How often do you quarrel?	0	2	53	43	2
How often does your wife get on your nerves?	1	2	53	41	3
Do you have regrets that you married your wife?	0	0	9	29	62
How often has your wife struck you in anger?	0	0	4	21	76
How often do you plan for the future together?	17	45	32	6	0
Do you confide in your wife?	32	46	18	4	1
How often do you feel satisfied in your marriage?	42	52	6	0	0
How often do you spend leisure time doing things with your wife?	11	53	32	4	1

Average marital quality score = 23.9

Question	All the Time	Most of the Time	Some of the Time	Hardly Ever	Never
Wives:					
How often do you quarrel?	0	4	46	46	4
How often does your husband get on your nerves?	2	5	56	36	1
Do you have regrets that you married your husband?	0	1	13	30	56
How often has your husband struck you in anger?	0	0	2	11	87
How often do you plan for the future together?	18	41	33	7	0
Do you confide in your husband?	40	44	14	1	1
How often do you feel satisfied with your marriage?	37	56	6	2	0
How often do you spend leisure time doing things with your husband?	18	53	22	7	0

Average marital quality score = 24.1

average score of both husbands and wives was approximately 24. Almost nobody scored in the lower half of the scale (16 or less). Fifty-three percent of the husbands and 50% of the wives scored between 17 and 24; 45% of the husbands and 47% of the wives had scores greater than 24. In sum, few people in this sample see their marriages in negative terms. About half perceive the quality of their marriages as neutral or mildly positive; another half perceive it as positive.

In addition to items in the marital quality scale, we asked participants about the love they felt for their spouses. Sixty-seven percent of the husbands and 65% of the wives reported that they felt a strong, intense love for their partners; 28% of the husbands and 27% of the wives said that their love was reasonably strong. Less than 10% felt that their love was moderately strong or not strong at all.

It appears that many people perceive the events in their marriages in fairly neutral terms but are satisfied with what they have. They rarely perceive anything negative about their marriages, but they see nothing positive about them. They don't quarrel and get on each other's nerves often, but they don't often plan for the future or spend leisure time together. At the same time they feel at least a reasonably strong love for their partners and are satisfied with the marriage, as if they are satisfied with the absence of pain.

Husbands and wives appear to perceive the quality of their marriages in much the same way; their summary scores are distributed almost identically. They express similar levels of love toward their partners and are equally satisfied with their marriages. Only minor differences appear within separate items.

DIFFERENCES BETWEEN SOCIOECONOMIC GROUPS

The major purpose of this chapter and the two that follow is to discover factors that will help us understand why some couples have better marriages than others. We are especially interested in examining the effects of factors related to managing two careers as well as a family. The couple's socioeconomic position is a reasonable place to begin that exploration.

In keeping with the research findings of earlier studies (Bahr et al., 1983; Huber and Spitze, 1980), we found that socioeconomic subgroups do not differ greatly in their perception of the quality of their marriages. Table 4.2 shows the average marital quality scores within different socioeconomic subgroups.

The quality of marriage as perceived by participants in the Work and Family Study does not differ, whether or not the wife works in the labor force. On the average, persons in marriages in which both partners are employed do not perceive their marriages as any worse or any better than persons in marriages in which only the husband is employed. Early research, which compared the marital satisfaction of employed and nonemployed women, concluded that when the wife works outside the home the couple, particularly the husband, experiences poorer marital adjustment (Axelson, 1963; Nye and Hoffman, 1963; Order and Bradburn, 1969). Later studies, however, were unable to replicate those findings and concluded that no relationship exists between a wife's employment and marital happiness (Booth, 1977; Glenn and Weaver, 1978; Wright, 1978). The data from the Work and Family Study agree with the more recent findings.

Better research or a change in society may explain why the early studies found a relationship between wife's employment and quality of marriage while later studies did not. The early studies were based on smaller samples, which were not always drawn to be representative; thus, the probability of error was larger. In addition, however, employment among wives has become accepted more widely. During the decade from 1972 to 1982, for example, participants in the General Social Survey conducted by the National Opinion Research Center (1986) showed an increase from 64% to 75% in support for married women's working. This wider acceptance of dual-earner marriages would reduce the strain caused by the wife's employment. It is also possible that marital selection may involve consideration of the

Table 4.2 Distribution of Marital Quality within Socioeconomic Categories, Score Means

	Perceived Marital Quality	
	Husband	Wife
Wife's Employment		
In labor force	23.8	24.0
Not in labor force	24.3	24.2
(Percentage of variance explained)	0.0	0.0
Husband's Education		
Less than high school graduate	24.1	23.1
High school graduate	23.8	23.5
More than high school graduate	23.9	24.3
(Percentage variance explained)	0.0	1.2
Husband's Occupation		
Professional-managerial	24.0	24.4
Clerical-sales	23.8	23.8
Service	24.2	23.8
Skilled	24.8	24.5
Semiskilled and unskilled	23.1	23.2
(Percentage variance explained)	2.0	1.4
Wife's Education		
Less than high school graduate	24.6	24.4
High school graduate	23.6	23.5
More than high school graduate	24.1	24.3
(Percentage variance explained)	0.8	0.9
Wife's Occupation		
Professional-managerial	24.0	24.2
Clerical-sales	23.7	24.0
Service	23.8	24.1
Skilled	24.8	24.8
Semiskilled and unskilled	23.0	22.2
(Percentage variance explained)	0.6	1.2
Traditional	23.8	24.2
Nontraditional	23.9	23.2
(Percentage variance explained)	0.0	1.4*
Family Income		
Less than $20,000	24.0	24.2
$20,000 to $29,000	23.9	24.0
$30,000 and above	23.9	24.0
(Percentage variance explained)	0.0	0.0
Relative Occupational Status		
Wife higher	23.8	23.4
Equal	23.5	24.0
Husband higher	24.0	24.2
(Percentage variance explained)	0.4	0.9

* $p < .05$

wife's employment. In earlier years, when wives were not expected to work, strain may have been created by the difference between what couples expected and what occurred. Now couples considering marriage can address their expectations about whether the wife will be employed and can resolve any conflict before marriage. In any case, participants in the Work and Family Study are consistent with those in other recent studies, who found that the wife's employment did not affect marital quality.

Some scholars argue that although the wife's employment is unrelated to the quality of marriage, her success might have some bearing (Parsons, 1942; Safilios-Rothschild, 1975). Successful women could endanger the security of men who see them as competitors, who find them unsubmissive, or whose masculinity is threatened by their own inability to play the dominant role. At the same time, successful women could have trouble balancing the "unfeminine" demands of succeeding occupationally with the "feminine" demands of being a wife. Despite what could be, however, participants in the Work and Family Study are not affected strongly by the wife's success. In fact, although the differences are minor, the lowest-quality marriages are perceived by both husbands and wives when the wives are employed in semiskilled and unskilled jobs. Among respondents in this sample the wife's achievement—either educational or occupational—does not reduce the quality of marriage as perceived by either spouse.

A more frequent argument on this subject suggests that marital quality is offered not by the wife's achievement per se, but by her achievement relative to her husband's (Becker, 1973; Hicks and Platt, 1970; Parsons, 1942; Santos, 1975). Several studies, however, discount the validity of these arguments. Oppenheimer (1977) analyzed the occurrence of divorce when wives' occupational statuses exceed those of their husbands; Huber and Spitze (1980) examined thoughts of divorce as affected by the relative incomes of husbands and of wives; Richardson (1979) explored the relationship between reported marital happiness and relative occupational achievements. All these scholars concluded that the quality of marriage is not reduced by the wife surpassing her husband in achievement. This study largely replicates those findings; although marital quality was perceived to be higher when the husband's occupational status surpassed his wife's, the differences are not large enough to be significant.

Analyses conducted by Hornung and McCullough (1981) and by Philliber and Hiller (1983) show that problems do occur in marriages when the wife's attainments are higher than her husband's. Hornung and McCullough (1981) found that achievement orientation functions as a contextual variable in the relationship between relative status and marital and life satisfaction. Both forms of satisfaction were less among men whose attainments were less than their wives' and among women whose attainments were greater than their husbands', but these relationships were stronger among people with high achievement orientation. Philliber and Hiller (1983) found that when a wife's occupational attainment surpasses her husband's, either the marriage is likely to result in divorce or the wife is likely to abandon her career for a job more compatible with her husband's. Such changes are most likely if she is employed in a position occupied traditionally by men. These findings suggest that other variables determine whether the spouses' relative attainments are a factor in the quality of marriage that they experience. We will discuss this question further in later chapters.

Here we examine the *direct* effect of a wife's employment in a traditional or a nontraditional occupation on the quality of marriage as perceived by each partner. In an earlier study (Philliber and Hiller, 1983) we found that women who were employed in nontraditional occupations, those held normally by men, were more likely to undergo negative marital and/or career changes during a seven-year period. In the Work and Family Study we recorded the percentage of women in each occupation in the Cincinnati metropolitan area. We classified the wife's occupation as traditional if the majority of people employed in that position were women and nontraditional if the majority were men. It appears that the distinction does not affect the quality of marriage as perceived by husbands, but it does make a difference to wives. Wives employed in jobs held normally by men experience lower-quality marriages.

A number of factors may explain the lower quality of marriages among women in nontraditional jobs. Their very presence in a nontraditional position may subject them to pressures that affect the quality of all their relationships. In addition, they may experience greater conflict with their husbands because they feel that they have violated his expectations or because they have expectations about him which he does not meet. We will explore these points further.

It has been argued as well that better-educated husbands and wives of higher socioeconomic status can cope better than less well-educated couples of lower socioeconomic status with the dual demands of a two-earner marriage and a family. Such people are believed to be less traditional and, thus, more able to adjust to new situations; education may perform a socialization function which prepares individuals to expect a two-earner marriage. Whatever arguments are proposed, however, they do not seem to apply to couples in the Work and Family Study. In this study the quality of marriages does not vary with the amount of education of either partner or with family income or husband's occupation.

Overall, socioeconomic variables do not make a difference in the perceived quality of couples' marriages. Neither the wife's level of attainment nor her attainment relative to her husband's is related strongly to the wife's or the husband's perception. Couples with lower education and less income perceive their marriages in the same way as better-educated, more affluent couples. Taken together, socioeconomic variables account for only 1.0% of the differences in quality of marriage observed by husbands and 3.3% of the differences observed by wives.

MARITAL QUALITY AND STAGES IN THE LIFE CYCLE

In the Work and Family Study life cycle variables appear to be more important than socioeconomic differences to the quality of marriages. People must deal with different problems and pressures at different points in their lives; these factors may affect

Table 4.3 Distribution of Marital Quality within Stages of the Life Cycle, Score Means

	Perceived Marital Quality	
	Husband	Wife
Number of Years Married		
Less than 5	24.3	24.9
5 to 9	22.9	23.6
10 or more	24.1	23.7
(Percentage variance explained)	2.2*	2.4*
Number of Children		
None	24.3	24.8
One	23.8	24.5
Two	23.6	23.6
Three or more	24.1	23.8
(Percentage variance explained)	0.7	1.6
Number of Children at Home		
None	24.6	24.6
One	24.1	24.2
Two	23.2	23.3
Three or more	23.7	24.0
(Percentage variance explained)	2.9*	1.7*
Age		
Under 30	23.4	24.4
30–49	23.8	23.9
50 and over	24.6	23.8
(Percentage variance explained)	1.9*	0.4

* $p < .05$

the quality of their relationships with significant others. Table 4.3 shows how some of these variables are related to husbands' and wives' perceptions of the quality of their relationships.

The number of years of marriage has a significant effect on perceptions of the quality of the marriage among both husbands and wives. Those who perceive their marriages as best have been married less than five years; those who perceive their marriages as poorest in quality have been married more than five years but less than 10. After 10 years, the perception of quality rises again. It may be that the first years of a marriage are regarded as a honeymoon period; the partners are fascinated with each other and are involved in discovery. After some time, however, the newness wears off and conflicts emerge; during this period the quality of the relationship declines. Some couples work through their problems and the quality presumably rises; others don't solve their problems, and they separate. Those who have divorced have fallen out of our sample of married couples. As a result, the perception of the quality of marriage is higher among people married at least 10 years than among those married more than 5 years but less than 10.

For both husbands and wives the amount of decline after 5 years of marriage is about the same. Husbands married more than 10 years, however, perceive their marriages as having approximately the same quality as do men married less than 5 years, whereas wives married more than 10 years continue to perceive a lower quality. This difference may be related less to the length of the marriage and more to age.

We found the older a husband is, the more favorably he perceives the quality of his marriage. For wives in this study the difference is not as great and is in the opposite direction. Older women have lived through a period of great transition, affecting their roles in the family. Before marrying they were led to expect a marriage to a man who would support them while they stayed home and raised children, like the women they knew. In reality, however, their husbands couldn't support them, and they had to stay in the labor force. They were older than their mothers had been when they began to bear children, and they had fewer children. Often those children were cared for by others. These older women served as role models for younger women; when the younger women married, their expectations conformed more closely to current reality. This match between younger women's expectations and experiences may account for the lower marital quality perceived by older women.

Younger men may have more difficulty than older men in establishing high-quality relationships that depend on emotional bonds. Younger men are involved deeply in establishing their identity as men, a process that involves greater development of instrumental skills than of emotional skills. It may be that men feel free to develop emotional relationships only after they become comfortable as men. If modern marriages depend more than in the past on meeting partners' emotional needs, older men would be expected to have higher-quality marriages.

The number of children born to a couple has little bearing on marital quality, but the number of children at home is important. Both husbands and wives who have no children living at home perceive a better relationship with their partners than do people with children at home. Children require time and are a priority that cannot be ignored. Their physical and emotional needs make constant demands on at least one parent. Although child rearing brings its own rewards, it reduces the time that partners can spend together. The relationship between the parents tends to be secondary to the children's demands.

The demands of one child do not appear to make much difference in the quality of marriage. Couples with only one child at home perceive their marriages as only a little lower in quality than do couples without children. The relationship between spouses deteriorates when two or more children are present.

Overall stages in the life cycle are related more closely than socioeconomic variables to differences in the perception of marital quality. The number of years of marriage and the number of children living at home affect the quality of marriage as perceived by both husbands and wives, although the effects are not the same. These variables, together with the age and number of children, explain 4.7% of the differences in the quality that husbands perceive in their marriages and 2.3% of the differences perceived by wives. Thus, the life cycle accounts for some of the differences in perception, but much remains unexplained.

SUMMARY

Data from the 489 couples who participated in the Work and Family Study provide some insight into the perceived quality of marriages. Very few people described their marriages negatively; this finding is consistent with the expectation that the primary basis for marriage in modern society is emotional gratification. Individuals who do not receive that gratification may well separate from their partners.

Although neither husbands nor wives perceive their marriages in negative terms, they vary in the positiveness of their perceptions. The responses of about one-half of the husbands and one-half of the wives fell into the lower part of the positive range of the measure of marital quality; the others fell into the upper part. The next question, then, is "What determines how positively people perceive the quality of their marriages?"

Socioeconomic variables do not appear to be related directly to either husbands' or wives' perceptions of the quality of marriage. It does not matter whether the wife is employed; if she is employed, her occupational achievement is unimportant both in absolute terms and relative to her husband. For wives, it does make some difference whether she is working in a job held normally by men or by women. Women in jobs held traditionally by men perceive lower quality in their marriages. The husband's occupation, his and his wife's education, and total family income are unrelated to the quality of marriage as perceived by either spouse.

Life cycle variables make some difference in people's perception of their marriages. The presence of children in the home reduces the quality of the relationship between husband and wife. Both husbands and wives describe high-quality relationships when they have been married less than 5 years and lower-quality relationships in the second 5 years of marriage. Men who have been married longer than 10 years perceive the quality of marriage much the same as recently married men, while women married longer than 10 years continue to have perceptions similar to those of women married from 5 to 10 years.

Neither socioeconomic nor life cycle variables are related strongly to differences in either husbands' or wives' perceptions of the quality of their marriages. Together these variables explain only 5.6% of the variation in quality for husbands and 5.3% for wives.

CHAPTER FIVE

Who Does What: Expectations and Realities

Although married women in the labor force are an established fact, the institutions of society still are geared to meet the needs of two-parent families with only one employed partner. Two outside jobs demand that couples take time to negotiate a household division of labor that once was a given; at the same time, employment absorbs more time and requires greater efficiency in performing household tasks. Within the family, equity and fairness in the distribution of costs and rewards become an issue. Partners may be overloaded with demands on their time and energy, and that pressure in turn may create rigid role expectations as well as emotional exhaustion. Such conditions could create an environment ripe for dissent.

People enter marriage with expectations about what they and their spouses should do. Although they are drawn together for emotional gratification, other tasks must be performed. Purchases must be made, meals prepared, laundry done, children cared for, bills paid. Individuals vary in their expectations about who should perform these tasks; they may expect to share each task or to divide the labor so that each spouse takes responsibility for particular tasks. If an individual believes that responsibility for tasks should be divided, he or she probably will also have some expectations about who should do which tasks most appropriately. In a traditional marriage, for example, men are expected to provide income and manage the family finances, while women are expected to take the responsibility for the homemaking and child care.

Rigid expectations about who should do what in a marriage may reduce the gratification for each partner. Individuals who hold traditional role expectations may have difficulty in adjusting to the discovery that the husband cannot earn enough income to provide the lifestyle that the couple desires, and both partners may come to view the husband as a failure. Similarly, the wife who works outside the home during the day and expects, or is expected, to retain primary responsibilty for homemaking and child care may find it difficult to adjust to a house that isn't always clean and children who want more time than they receive. These expectations not only set up conflicts regarding the adequacy of the individuals expected to perform the roles; they also reduce the couple's ability to accomplish the tasks. Perhaps some tasks, such as child care, can be performed better if they are shared. Because time is the critical factor, involvement by both spouses increases the available time. Other tasks perhaps can be performed better by the person who is not expected to do them. The family will suffer if the wife is the better money manager but only if the husband is expected to take that responsibility. The husband's schedule may make it easier for him to buy the family groceries, but that option is not open if the couple believes that grocery shopping is the wife's responsibility. Ultimately these role expectations limit the family's flexibility.

Although a division of labor in the home may increase the efficiency with which tasks are done, it also may reduce the spouses' ability to meet each other's emotional needs. If both spouses share responsibility for a variety of tasks, they must communicate with one another constantly to ensure that those tasks are done. Constant monitoring is required to make sure that groceries are bought, children are picked up, meals are prepared, and laundry is done. This monitoring takes time and so reduces the efficiency in completing these tasks, but the communication between spouses creates a basis for sharing and for meeting emotional needs as well. In short, a successful division of labor within a marriage may be so efficient that spouses are not required to talk to each other to get things done. Marital partners who have less clearly defined role expectations may be more flexible in meeting the family's instrumental needs, at the same time developing an emotionally supportive and gratifying relationship with each family member.

Marital partners who attempt to maintain a traditional division of labor in the home while both are employed may develop an imbalanced relationship in which one partner's contributions outweigh those of the other. In a traditional marriage the relationship between husband and wife is complementary; husbands provide the necessary income and wives provide a home. This exchange makes each person a valued partner in the relationship. In contrast, this complementarity may be absent in marriages in which the wife earns a substantial portion of the family income while also maintaining primary responsibility for traditional homemaking and childcare tasks. Wives may feel exploited because they contribute more to the relationship than they receive. In turn, husbands may feel an obligation that they are unable to meet; they need their wives more than their wives need them.

The decline of traditional roles within the family may have created a new problem for some couples. Traditional roles segregated husbands' and wives' activities, allowing each to be successful in their own areas without encouraging comparisons. When both partners pursue occupational careers, however, they make comparisons regarding which partner is the more successful. If the couple also shares tasks within the home, they make judgments about which is the better parent, and similar matters. Competitive individuals who need to outdo others may feel threatened when they find their marital partners more successful than themselves, or they may look down on a less successful spouse who fails to provide good competition. The ability to give and receive emotional gratification in such a relationship will be threatened seriously.

THE DIVISION OF LABOR

In the Work and Family Study we questioned husbands and wives on their expectations about who should be responsible for child care, housework, money management, and income earning. The first two tasks are associated traditionally with wives and the second two with husbands. Each person was asked to state whether these tasks should be performed entirely or mostly by themselves, by both partners equally, or mostly or entirely by spouses. The result was that those who thought that tasks should not be performed equally also thought that husbands should earn income and manage finances while wives should do housework and take care of the children.

Table 5.1 shows husbands' and wives' expectations about who should do what in a marriage. Of the two tasks associated traditionally with women, almost all husbands and wives agreed that child care should be a shared responsibility. Only about half of the respondents felt that housework should be shared, however; half of the wives and almost half of the husbands felt that it should be done by the wife. These findings show a normative, almost universal expectation that parenting is the responsibility of both mothers and fathers, but the same norm does not exist in regard to housework. Both husbands and wives are divided almost equally over whether housework should be shared or done primarily by the wife. Interestingly, more wives than husbands believe that it should be the wife's job.

Of tasks performed traditionally by men, 40% of the couples in the study agree that both partners should decide how to spend money, but only about one-fourth agree that earning money should be shared. The majority continues to believe that providing for the family should be the husband's responsibility.

When couples disagree, spouses who traditionally perform a given role believe that they should continue to do so, while their

Table 5.1 Expectations about Performance of Marital Roles,
in Percentages

	Task should be done . . .		
	by wife	*by both*	*by husband*
Child care			
Husband	9	90	1
Wife	10	90	0
Percentage of agreement by both: 82 by wife: 2			
Housework			
Husband	43	54	3
Wife	50	50	0
Percentage of agreement by both: 36 by wife: 30			
Money management			
Husband	14	60	26
Wife	18	68	14
Percentage of agreement by both: 43 by husband: 1			
Income earning			
Husband	1	31	68
Wife	1	47	52
Percentage of agreement by both: 23 by husband: 43			

partners believe that those tasks should be shared. Husbands
are more likely to believe that they alone should be responsible
for earning and managing money, while wives are more likely to
believe that they alone should be responsible for domestic matters. This finding suggests that few husbands or wives want to
give up the prerogatives attached to their traditional marital
roles, but that some are interested in expanding their activities
into nontraditional areas.

Table 5.2 Accuracy of Spouse's Perception of Partner's Expectations, in Percentages

	Accuracy of Wife's Perception			Accuracy of Husband's Perception		
	Husband more traditional	Perception accurate	Husband less traditional	Wife more traditional	Perception accurate	Wife less traditional
Having a working wife	26	38	36			
Child care	6	73	21	11	82	7
Housework	9	55	36	27	65	8
Managing money	37	44	19	18	51	31
Earning income	22	55	23	13	61	26

Expectations and Perceptions of Expectations

When people's expectations are compared to their spouses' perceptions of those expectations, it appears that spouses misperceive their partner's expectations fairly often. We asked participants what they thought their spouses' expectations were with respect to each of the four tasks: child care, housework, money management, and income earning. In addition, husbands were asked how they felt about their wives working for pay, and wives were asked what they thought their husbands felt. The findings in Table 5.2 show that in five of the nine comparisons, over 40% of the respondents had inaccurate perceptions of their partners' expectations; in two of those comparisons (wife's perception of husband's attitude about her working and about who should manage money) the majority were incorrect. Husbands' perceptions about their wives' expectations were more accurate than the reverse. On each of the four items asked of both husbands and wives, husbands were accurate more often than wives.

Errors in perceptions about housekeeping and child care occur most often when husbands are less traditional and wives are more traditional than their partners expect. More wives believe that husbands have more traditional expectations than they actually do; they believe that their husbands expect them to do housework and care for the children when, in fact, their husbands believe that these roles should be shared. At the same time, more husbands believe that wives have less traditional expectations than they actually do. They believe that their wives expect them to share housework and child care when, in fact, wives do not expect this.

Inaccuracies in the perceptions of expectations for roles assigned traditionally to men occur most often when wives are less traditional and husbands are more traditional than their partners expect. Wives more often perceive husbands' expectations about managing money to be less traditional than they actually are, but they misperceive husbands' expectations about earning money approximately equally in both directions. Husbands more often perceive wives' expectations about both managing and earning money to be more traditional than they actually are.

Perceptions of Who Does What

Participants in the study were presented with a list of 20 household and child-care tasks and asked whether these tasks were done mostly by themselves, mostly by their spouses, equally by both, or by others. The results indicate a major discrepancy between expectations and behavior. Although 58% of the husbands say that housework should be shared, Table 5.3 shows that except for two tasks, not more than one-third of the husbands either share housework or do it regularly, even by their own estimate. More husbands shop for food and do dishes than perform other tasks.

The percentage of wives who perceive their husbands as doing or sharing tasks is lower than the percentage of husbands who perceive themselves as doing them. Both husbands and

Table 5.3 Husband's and Wife's Perceptions of Division of Labor, in Percentages

	Wife's Perception			Husband's Perception			Agreement between Spouses
	Wife does	Both do	Husband does	Wife does	Both do	Husband does	
Regular Household Tasks							
Food shopping	70	20	10	67	23	10	86
Meal preparation	85	10	5	82	13	5	81
House cleaning	80	17	3	73	23	4	78
Washing dishes	66	29	5	57	36	7	87
Washing clothes	84	10	6	81	14	5	76
Ironing	90	7	3	90	7	3	90
Managing money	42	31	27	30	38	32	65
Less Regular Household Tasks							
Household repairs	7	13	80	2	7	91	82
Yard work	11	29	60	6	24	70	71
Supervision of help	72	24	4	51	34	15	56
Entertainment preparation	52	46	2	44	53	3	61
Major purchases	14	82	4	9	85	6	79
Planning recreation	16	80	4	11	83	7	72
Planning vacations	8	85	7	8	82	10	79
Child Care Tasks							
Arranging activities	61	36	3	58	40	2	63
Taking children to doctor	74	23	3	62	34	4	73
Getting children ready for bed	60	34	6	48	47	5	71
Getting children ready for school	82	11	7	80	16	4	81
Helping children with homework	45	41	14	35	54	11	65
Staying home when children are sick	62	36	2	48	48	4	52

wives report that money management is the only regular household task that a majority of husbands either does or shares.

Although wives perform the more regular household tasks, a number of husbands do household tasks that are less regular or are needed only occasionally. Almost all husbands take primary responsibility for household repairs and yard work; a large proportion also shares in making major purchases, planning recreation, and planning vacations. Many also share in supervising help and in preparing for entertainment.

Although 84% of all couples with children at home agree that child care should be shared, half or more of the fathers participate equally or more in only three of the six child-care tasks: staying with sick children, getting children ready for bed, and helping children with homework. Wives believe that only about one-third of their husbands participate equally or more in any child care tasks, except for helping with homework.

Generally couples agree about who does what around the house. With the exception of money management, at least three-quarters agree about whether regular household tasks are done primarily by the wife or by the husband, or are shared. They agree less about who does nonregular household tasks and even less about who performs child-care tasks, but the majority of couples agree on every task. Across the board, both husbands and wives see themselves as participating more than their spouses believe they participate. Husbands especially are more likely to see tasks as shared while wives see themselves as having major responsibility.

SOCIOECONOMIC AND LIFE CYCLE EFFECTS ON THE DIVISION OF LABOR

We created summary scales to see how socioeconomic and life cycle differences are related to expectations and reports about the division of labor. We created measures of expectations of role performance by assigning values from 1 to 4, with 4 corresponding to the most traditional response: husbands should be entirely responsible for earning income and managing money, while wives should be entirely responsible for housekeeping and child care. We then summed scores across responses to create a scale from 0 to 16, with 16 representing the most traditional expectations. In the same manner we created a scale for perceptions of spouse's expectations.

We created a summary measure of the division of labor by counting the number of tasks (out of 20) for which the husband had primary responsibility or which he shared with his wife. If a given task was not performed by either spouse (e.g., if they performed no child-care tasks because they had no children), the individual's average was assigned to that item to make the scale comparable across individuals. Table 5.4 shows the mean expectations of role performance, perception of spouse's expectations, and perception of the division of labor within socioeconomic and life cycle subgroups for both husbands and wives.

Wife's employment is the variable which is related most strongly to expectations and reports about the division of labor. If the wife is in the labor force (either employed or looking for work), both husbands and wives report significantly higher traditional role expectations and perceptions of spouse's expectations, and report that the husband performs fewer household tasks. Differences in the wife's expectations are even greater than in the husband's.

These findings raise an issue that is beyond the ability of the data to explain. One possible explanation for these differences is that a marital selection process is in operation whereby people who hold traditional expectations enter marriages in which they establish a traditional division of labor that is satisfactory to both spouses. The other possibility is that individuals change their expectations to match the reality of the situation. In either case the fact that dual-earner couples maintain less traditional expectations and less rigid divisions of labor than single-earner couples helps explain why the wife's employment is unrelated to the perceived quality of the marriage.

The other two socioeconomic variables reported in Table 5.4 show much weaker relationships either to expectations or to

Table 5.4 Relationship of Expectations of Role Performance, Perceptions of Spouse's Expectations, and Perception of Division of Labor with Selected Socioeconomic and Life Cycle Variables

	Expectations of role performance		Perceptions of spouse's expectations		Perception of division of labor	
	Husband	Wife	Husband	Wife	Husband	Wife
Wife's Employment						
In labor force	9.1	8.8	8.9	8.8	11.9	10.7
Not in labor force	10.3	10.0	10.0	10.1	9.3	8.3
(Percentage variance explained)	(13%)*	(19%)*	(12%)*	(19%)*	(12%)*	(9%)*
Education						
Less than high school	9.1	10.0	9.0	9.9	11.1	8.6
High school	9.5	9.3	9.2	9.9	11.0	9.7
More than high school	9.4	8.9	9.2	9.5	11.3	10.5
(Percentage variance explained)	(1%)	(5%)*	(1%)	(2%)*	(0%)	(3%)*
Family Income						
Less than $20,000	9.5	9.3	9.2	9.8	12.0	10.4
$20,000–$30,000	9.6	9.3	9.0	9.8	11.5	10.0
$30,000 and above	9.4	9.0	9.2	9.6	11.1	10.1
(Percentage variance explained)	(0%)	(1%)	(0%)	(0%)	(1%)	(0%)
Age						
Less than 30	9.3	8.8	9.0	9.6	12.4	11.0
30 to 49	9.4	9.2	9.2	9.7	11.2	9.7
50 and above	9.5	9.4	9.5	9.8	10.2	9.7
(Percentage variance explained)	(0%)	(4%)*	(2%)*	(0%)	(6%)*	(3%)*
Years Married						
Less than 5	9.1	8.8	8.9	9.5	12.5	11.0
5 to 9	9.5	9.1	9.0	9.8	11.5	10.2
10 or more	9.5	9.3	9.5	9.8	10.4	9.5
(Percentage variance explained)	(2%)*	(3%)*	(4%)*	(1%)	(9%)*	(3%)*
Children at Home						
None	9.2	8.8	9.1	9.5	11.7	11.1
One	9.4	9.2	9.2	9.7	11.4	9.9
Two	9.5	9.4	9.2	9.9	10.8	9.4
Three or more	9.7	9.4	9.0	9.7	10.7	9.4
(Percentage variance explained)	(2%)*	(4%)*	(1%)	(1%)	(2%)*	(5%)*

* $p < .05$

practice in the division of labor. The level of family income is unrelated to these variables for both husbands and wives; on the average, individuals at all levels hold the same expectations and practice the same division of labor. The husband's education does not affect his expectations or perceptions of the division, but the wife's education makes some differences. On the average, the lower the wife's educational level, the more traditional her expectations, the more traditional she perceives her husband's expectations to be, and the fewer household tasks she perceives her husband as doing.

The husband's education, however, is unrelated to his expectations and performance of roles. In general, education is expected to produce less traditional individuals, but in this case it does not matter. It may well be that more egalitarian norms are spreading throughout society so that earlier differences related to education now have disappeared.

Each of the life cycle variables (age, years married, and number of children at home) shows some relationship to expectations and practices, although none of the differences are great. The older the individuals are, the longer they have been married, and the more children they have living at home, the more traditional their expectations and the fewer household tasks the husband performs. Older individuals, who probably have been married longer, established their marriages at a time when a traditional division of labor was the norm. Younger individuals entered marriages with the expectation that both would earn income and perhaps that both would share tasks around the home. These couples also are most likely to have delayed starting a family; this fact may account for the finding that the husband appears to do more around the home in families with fewer children.

EFFECTS OF THE DIVISION OF LABOR ON MARITAL QUALITY

In order to see how people's expectations, their perceptions of their spouses' expectations, and the division of labor in the

Table 5.5 Effect of Expectations of Role Performance, Perceptions of Spouses' Expectations, and Perception of Division of Labor on Quality of Marriage, Standardized Coefficients

| | Marital Quality | | | |
| | Husband | | Wife | |
	Wife in labor force	Wife not in labor force	Wife in labor force	Wife not in labor force
Husband's expectations	−.13*	.10	−.01	.22
Wife's expectations	.11	.13	.15*	.26*
Husband's perception of wife's expectations	.06	−.09	.07	.18
Wife's perception of husband's expectations	−.13*	−.19	−.21*	−.28*
Division of labor	.18*	.15	.25*	.28*
(Percentage variance explained)	8	5	12	14

* $p < .05$

home are related to the quality of marriage perceived by each partner, we entered the measures of each variable into a simultaneous regression equation. The results, displayed in Table 5.5, show the relative effect of each variable for husbands and for wives. Findings are presented separately for couples in which the wife belongs to the labor force and in which she does not.

It appears immediately that expectations and practices surrounding role divisions are more important than either socioeconomic or life cycle variables in the quality of marriage as perceived by the partners. Five percent of the variance is explained for husbands whose wives do not belong to the labor force; 8% is explained for husbands whose wives do belong. For wives the respective percentages are 14% and 12%, more than twice as great as the effect of socioeconomic and life cycle variables.

Whether or not the wife is employed, a major factor contributing to the quality of marriage for both husbands and wives is the amount of work done by the husband in the home. The more tasks the husband shares with his wife or does himself, the higher the quality of marriage perceived by both partners. Wives especially perceive their marriages as better when their husbands are involved around the home. Families that adhere to a strict division of labor, with the husband providing income and the wife providing housework and child care, experience lower-quality marriages even if the wife is not part of the labor force.

It is important that the husband's expectations be consistent with his wife's employment. The more traditional his expectations, the lower the quality of marriage he experiences if his wife is in the labor force. That is, if the husband believes that he should be the one to provide the income while his wife takes care of the home and the children, he experiences a less satisfactory marriage. On the other hand, if the husband has traditional expectations and if the wife is not in the labor force, both the husband and the wife report higher-quality marriages.

For both dual-earner couples and couples in which only the husband belongs to the labor force, husbands and wives alike, especially wives, experience higher-quality marriages if the wife's expectations are more traditional. It is hard to know exactly what this finding means; it may imply that it is all right for a wife to have a job as long as she does not take it too seriously. Both she and her husband are happier when she expects to take primary responsibility for the home and the children and expects her husband to take primary responsibility for earning and managing money. When she believes that she should share responsibility for earning and managing money and/or that he should share responsibility for the home and the children, the perceived quality of marriage is lower.

The more traditional the wife believes her husband's expectations to be, the lower the quality of marriage experienced by both partners, whatever the husband does or expects. The effect is even greater for couples when the wife is not in the labor force than when she is. Wives' and husbands' expectations are less important than wives' perceptions of their husbands' expectations. It is one thing to live according to traditional role definitions; apparently it is quite another to feel that one is expected to do so.

SUMMARY

Among the respondents in the Work and Family Study, couples who expect and adhere rigidly to traditional divisions of labor are uncommon. Almost everyone believes that both parents should share responsibility for child care; large majorities believe that the management of money should be shared. Almost half, however, continue to believe that housework should be done primarily by the wife; over half believe that earning income is primarily the husband's responsibility.

In reality, the division of labor is more rigid than the expectations expressed. Except for managing money, only about one-third of the husbands, by their own report, share any regular household task. Taking care of the house from day to day is the wife's business.

Husbands do share responsibility for child care and perform household tasks that are required only occasionally. They take care of repairs and yard work and share in the planning of entertainment and recreation. About half of those who have children at home help with child care. Although this proportion is far less than the 90% who said that they believed child care should be shared, still it is substantial.

In general, expectations about the performance of roles and participation in various tasks are unrelated to socioeconomic and life cycle variables. The major exception is the wife's participation in the labor force; both husbands and wives in dual-earner marriages report less traditional role expectations and greater participation by the husband in household tasks.

How spouses believe that roles should be divided and how those roles actually are divided have important consequences for the quality of marriage as experienced by husbands and by wives. Whether or not the wife is in the labor force, both partners report better marriages when the wife's expectations are more traditional but when she perceives her husband's expectations as less traditional. It is important that the husband's expectations match his wife's labor-force participation. If she is not in the labor force, a higher-quality marriage occurs when his expectations are more traditional; if she belongs to the labor force, the quality of marriage is higher when his expectations are less traditional. Yet no matter what the expectations are, both husbands and wives consistently report higher-quality marriages when the husband performs or shares more tasks.

Throughout this book we assume that expectations and other social psychological attitudes such as competitiveness, perceptions of imbalance, and gender-role identities are causal variables affecting quality of marriage and the relationship between that quality and the occupational attainments of spouses. In reality those relationships are probably reciprocal. That is to say, people probably change their expectations and other attitudes to be consistent with what is going on. Also, people who are experiencing a higher quality marriage, for whatever reason, may change other attitudes as a result of that high quality experience. Marriages in which those changes do not take place may disintegrate and fall beyond the purview of this sample. It is clearly outside the ability of these cross sectional data to untangle relationships of that complexity. What we can be sure of is that certain attitudes and behaviors appear to be associated with perceptions of higher quality marriages on the part of husbands and wives.

CHAPTER SIX

Consequences of Competitiveness, Imbalance, and Gender-Role Identity

The three most prominent perspectives predicting negative consequences from a wife's participation in the labor force emphasize the effects of competitiveness, imbalance, and gender-role identity. Talcott Parsons (1942, 1943) was among the first to argue that competition was created by both spouses' participation in the labor force. He believed that in traditional marriages, with the husband employed and the wife taking care of the home and the children, both partners were able to be the best in the family at what they did. When both the husband and the wife had careers, however, others might make comparisons between them and judge one to be superior to the other. Marriages are held together by the emotional bonds that exist between husbands and wives; competition weakens those bonds, reducing the quality of the marital experience.

Gary Becker (1973) believes that dual-earner marriages create problems because they disturb the balance in a traditional relationship. When the husband is responsible for producing income and the wife is responsible for the home and the children, each partner contributes something unique to the relationship, at the same time depending on a spouse to supply what he or she does not provide. When the wife enters the labor force and begins to produce income that is a significant part of the family budget, an imbalance is created in the relationship. The wife may contribute more to the relationship than she receives, especially when she continues to have primary responsibility for housekeeping and child care. As a result she may feel exploited and become resentful. The husband is in the opposite position; he receives more than he contributes. He may need his wife to provide housekeeping and child care more than she needs him to provide income, and he may feel trapped in a relationship where he cannot provide his share. If he can share housekeeping and child-care responsibilities while his wife earns a substantial amount of the family income, the interdependency found in a traditional marriage no longer exists. The partners lead parallel lives; at any point each is capable of living apart from the other. In that event, balance is no longer an issue.

The third perspective that predicts negative consequences in dual-earner marriages focuses on the threat to self-concepts. The development of a self-concept incorporates gender-role identities, in which people perceive themselves as more or less masculine and more or less feminine. A masculine gender-role identity stresses the importance of being dominant and forceful, and acting as a leader. A feminine gender-role identity emphasizes the importance of being sensitive sympathetic, understanding, and compassionate (Hiller and Philliber, 1985). According to Constantina Safilios-Rothschild (1975), a man who has a strong masculine and a weak feminine role identity is threatened by his wife's employment because his feelings of masculinity require him to be the one who provides for his family. The more the family depends on the wife's earnings, the greater the threat. The wife's situation is similar. If she has a high feminine and a low masculine role identity, and finds that she must earn money so that the family can have a desirable lifestyle, her femininity is threatened because she was unable to attract a man who could provide for her at some desired level. Each partner's behavior is inconsistent with what they believe they should be.

We measured competitiveness in the Work and Family Study

Table 6.1 Differences in Quality of Marriage for Husbands and Wives by Degree of Competitiveness, Perception of Balance, Gender-Role Identity, and Support for Wife Working

	Husband		Wife	
	Low	High	Low	High
Husband's Attitudes				
Competitiveness	24.2	23.7	24.3	23.8
Perception of balance	24.0	23.8	24.0	24.1
Assertiveness	23.8	24.1	24.2	23.9
Sensitivity	23.2	24.7*	23.6	24.5*
Support for wife working	23.6	24.2	23.6	24.5*
Wife's Attitudes				
Competitiveness	24.1	23.7	24.4	23.7*
Perception of balance	24.1	23.8	24.3	23.9
Assertiveness	24.2	23.6*	24.0	24.1
Sensitivity	23.8	24.1	23.6	24.6*
Perception of husband's support	23.7	24.2	23.6	24.5*

* p<.05

by asking participants how important it was to be better than their spouses at housekeeping, child care, income earning, and money management. Responses were summed across questions to form a scale ranging from 0 to 12, with a higher number indicating more competitiveness. Table 6.1 compares the quality of marriage experienced by people with below-average and above-average competitiveness.

If the Parsonian position is correct, marital quality should be lower when either husbands or wives need to be better than their spouses. Table 6.1, however, shows that the direct effects of competitiveness are not great. Although the average marital quality is a little higher when either spouse is below average in competitiveness, the differences are small. A wife's above-average competitiveness has a significant negative relationship to her marital quality, while her husband's competitiveness is not a factor in the marital quality she experiences.

To determine whether the perception of balance affected the perception of marital quality, we asked participants who was better at housekeeping, child care, income earning, and money management. We formed a summary scale, with a high number indicating a more balanced relationship. This variable is different from what Becker (1977) conceptualized in that Becker wrote about a structural imbalance while these questions measure the perception of imbalance. We have further complicated the situation by asking who was better at a task and not who actually does it. On the first point, it is reasonable to argue that what is important is what is perceived. On the second point, it is not enough to merely do a task; mutual dependency is created when one is better than the other at some, but not all, things. In a balanced relationship, the husband should be better at some things and the wife at others. Among participants in the study, however, we found that marital quality as experienced by either the husband or the wife was not influenced by the presence or the absence of balance.

We measured gender-role identities by asking participants how strongly they identified with the 20 masculine and 20 feminine traits identified by Bem (1974). Responses were summed to create separate scales for each role construct. In an earlier analysis of this data (Hiller and Philliber, 1985) we used the full scales as well as the primary factors in each (assertiveness in the masculinity scale and sensitivity in the femininity scale) as correlates with certain behaviors and attitudes. There were no differences in the outcomes. We believe the Bem scales measure two clusters of personality traits (assertiveness and sensitivity), which are both present in most men and women. Therefore, it seems most appropriate to refer to these constructs by their nonsexist labels, assertiveness or sensitivity. We will speak of gender-role identity in these terms from this point forward. The means displayed in Table 6.1 show that the more a husband shows traits of sensitivity, the more positive the marital experience is for both husbands and wives. The extent to which he demonstrates his assertiveness, however, does not affect the marriage.

The wife's demonstration of assertiveness affects the marriage, but in a negative direction. The more assertive she perceives herself to be, the lower the marital quality perceived by

Table 6.2 Relative Effects of Competitiveness, Balance, Gender-Role
Identity, and Support on Husbands' and Wives' Marital Quality,
Standardized Regression Coefficients

	Husband	*Wife*
Husband's Attitudes		
Competitiveness	−.12*	−.12*
Perception of balance	.03	.13*
Assertiveness	.04	−.01
Sensitivity	.30*	.17*
Support for wife working	.00	.03
Wife's Attitudes		
Competitiveness	−.08	−.14*
Perception of balance	−.04	−.07
Assertiveness	−.13*	−.02
Sensitivity	.08	.19*
Perception of husband's support	−.01	.04
Percentage of Variance Explained	.13	.11

* p<.05

the husband. The higher her sensitivity, however, the higher the
quality of marriage she perceives.

In addition to asking about competitiveness, balance, and
gender-role identity, we asked husbands about their support for
wives working and we asked wives about their perception of
that support. The findings reveal that both elements are important in the wives' perceived marital quality but not in the husbands'. In general, the more supportive a husband is and the
more supportive his wife perceives him to be, the higher the
marital quality experienced by the wife.

To examine the relative importance of competitiveness, balance, gender-role identity, and support, we entered these variables into simultaneous equations. The standardized coefficients
allow us to make comparisons between variables in order to see
which variables have the greatest effect on marital quality.

By far the most important factor affecting husbands' perceived marital quality is sensitivity. The stronger his sensitivity,
the more positive his perceived marital quality. The wife's per-

ceived marital quality also rises with the increase in the husband's sensitivity. His assertiveness, however, is not important to either spouse's marital quality. If we accept the scale of masculine role identity as a measure of assertiveness and instrumentality and the scale of feminine role identity as a measure of sensitivity and supportiveness, we can understand why the latter may be more important than the former in affecting the quality of a marital relationship. The contemporary marriage is based on the emotional attachment of two persons, and that attachment is expressed by giving and receiving emotional support. People who lack the ability to form emotional attachments by expressing love and support obviously will experience a lower-quality marital relationship than people who have that ability.

Both a husband's and a wife's sensitivity are related to marital quality as perceived by wives. It may well be that the husband takes for granted his wife's ability to give support because that ability is thought to be a common characteristic among women. For that reason he is not affected by his wife's level of sensitivity. The wife, however, is responsive to her husband's sensitivity as well as to her own attributes. The marital quality that she experiences is affected by her ability to be sensitive and supportive as well as by a husband who can be sensitive and supportive.

Although the husband's assertiveness is unimportant to both spouses' perceived marital quality, a stronger assertiveness score for the wife leads to a lower perceived marital quality for the husband. In general it appears that men have an adverse reaction to women who are more instrumental and forceful.

In this analysis of relative effects, the marital quality of both partners is affected negatively by the extent to which either the husband or the wife needs to be better than the other. Competitiveness is incompatible with a relationship that depends on two individuals' attachment to each other. That attachment is built on sharing and valuing the partner; feelings that one person is better than the other, or needs to be better than the other, are not consistent with that bond.

Perceptions about whether the relationship is balanced do not affect husbands' perceived marital quality. The more balanced the husband perceives the relationship to be, however, the more positive the marital quality experienced by the wife. If the husband feels dependent on his wife or if he feels that his wife is not doing her fair share, he might well send negative messages. The presence or absence of these messages may affect the quality of marriage she experiences.

In general it appears that wives respond more to their husbands' attitudes than the reverse. The wife's perceived marital quality is greater if her husband's sensitivity is stronger and if he perceives their relationship to be more balanced. The more competitive the husband, the poorer the quality of the marriage as perceived by the wife. Among the wife's attitudes, the husband is affected only by her assertiveness. Otherwise he is affected more strongly by his own traits.

EFFECTS OF WIFE'S EMPLOYMENT

Competitiveness, balance, gender-role identity, and husband's support for wife's employment may affect marital quality in one way when the wife is employed and in another way when she is not. In particular, the attitudes that support wives' working may be more important when the wife is employed than when she is not. We analyzed the effects of other variables on the quality of marital relationships separately for employed and for nonemployed wives. We determined the significance of the interactions by calculating interaction terms for each variable (wife's employment scores—0 or 1—times the value of the variable) and by entering each value into the equation to see whether there was a significant increase in the variance explained. Table 6.3 shows the unstandardized coefficients to enable a comparison between the effects when the wife is in the labor force and when she is not.

We note some important similarities in the effects of husbands' attitudes on the quality of marriage both when the wife is in the labor force and when she is not. Regardless of the wife's employment status, both husbands and wives experience lower

Table 6.3 Relative Effects of Competitiveness, Balance, Gender-Role Identity and Support on Husbands' and Wives' Marital Quality by Wife's Participation in the Labor Force, Unstandardized Regression Coefficients

	Wife in Labor Force (N=362)		Wife not in Labor Force (N=127)	
	Husband	Wife	Husband	Wife
Husband's Attitudes				
Competitiveness	−.13	−.17	−.12	−.14
Perception of balance	.04	.21	−.12*	−.04*
Assertiveness	−.01	−.01	.09	−.03
Sensitivity	.20	.11	.14	.12
Support for wife working	.06	.03	−.10*	.03
Wife's Attitudes				
Competitiveness	−.13	−.20	.04*	.07*
Perception of balance	−.06	−.12	−.17	−.04
Assertiveness	−.08	−.01	.03*	.08*
Sensitivity	.03	.12	.07	.17
Perception of husband's support	.08	.04	−.09*	−.15*
Percentage of Variance Explained	.17	.16	.20	.17

*Differs significantly when wife is in the labor force.

marital quality when the husband's competitiveness creates the need to be better than his wife. Both partners experience higher marital quality if the husband's sensitivity is stronger; his assertiveness remains unimportant. Once again, the data are consistent with the interpretation that a supportive husband is a critical factor in marital quality. Such a husband has the flexibility needed to support a wife emotionally in both traditional and nontraditional situations. Receiving that support improves the quality of marriage for her; giving that support improves the quality for him.

We also find important differences in the effects of husbands' attitudes on marital quality, depending on the wife's employment status. These factors differ not only in degree but also in direction. The more balanced the husband perceives the relationship to be, the higher the marital quality perceived by both spouses when the wife is in the labor force; the perceived marital quality is lower, however, when the wife is not in the labor force. When the wife is in the labor force, it is most important that the husband not feel threatened. In that case his perception of balance is important to her marital quality, but balance is not important to the wife when she is not in the labor force.

For obvious reasons the husband is affected negatively when he supports his wife's participation in the labor force and when she does not participate. His expectations are inconsistent with the reality of the situation.

The wife's attitudes also affect both spouses' perceived marital quality in different ways, depending on her participation in the labor force. If the wife has a need to be better than her husband, her competitiveness has negative effects on marital quality when she participates in the labor force but no effect when she does not. When the wife is in the labor force, the division of labor is reduced because both partners are participating in the same market. Their achievements can be compared easily. If the wife has a need to surpass her husband in these comparisons, the quality of their relationship is impaired. If she does not participate in the labor force, she can achieve in areas in which she is not in competition with her husband.

A wife's assertiveness has negative effects on the marital quality perceived by the husband (Table 6.2), but these effects appear to be limited to couples in which the wife is in the labor force. When the wife is not in the labor force, her assertiveness is unimportant to the husband but enhances her own perceived marital quality. If the wife has a strong, dominant personality and participates in the labor force, the situation appears to make the husband uncomfortable. She appears to benefit from those traits, however, as long as she is not in the labor force.

The wife's perception of her husband's support for her working has expected effects, depending on her employment. If the wife perceives that her husband wants her to participate in the labor force and she does not participate, that situation has a negative effect on the marital quality experienced by both partners.

Table 6.4 Relative Effects of Competitiveness, Balance, Gender-Role Identity, and Support on Husbands' and Wives' Marital Quality, by Wife's Relative Occupational Attainment, Unstandardized Regression Coefficients

| | Wife's Attainment Higher (N=128) | | Wife's Attainment Not Higher (N=231) | |
	Husband	Wife	Husband	Wife
Husband's Attitudes				
Competitiveness	−.09	−.23	−.17	−.04*
Perception of balance	−.05	.37	.12*	.22*
Assertiveness	.03	.08	−.04	−.07
Sensitivity	.22	.12	.18	.11
Support for wife working	−.11	−.08	.12*	.10*
Wife's Attitudes				
Competitiveness	−.03	−.17	−.19	−.31
Perception of balance	−.05	−.37	−.05	−.25
Assertiveness	−.04	−.15	−.09	.00*
Sensitivity	.01	.06	.04	.11
Perception of husband's support	.04	.13	.13	.21
Percentage of Variance Explained	.20	.24	.20	.19

*Differs significantly when wife's attainment is higher.

EFFECTS OF RELATIVE OCCUPATIONAL ATTAINMENTS

Table 6.4 compares the effects of competitiveness, balance, gender-role identity, and support when the wife's occupational attainment exceeds her husband's and when it does not. In general the differences related to relative occupational achievements are not as dramatic as those related to participation in the labor force, but a few interesting comparisons emerge.

If the husband has a need to surpass his wife and if the wife turns out to be the higher achiever, the marital quality perceived by the wife is lowered. The husband's competitiveness does not affect the wife, however, when he surpasses her. Once again the wife appears to respond to the husband's feelings and to develop negative perceptions when her behavior does not seem consistent with his feelings.

Relative attainment determines how the husband's perception of balance is related to marital quality. Perception of balance is unrelated to the husband's perceived marital quality when the wife's attainment is greater than his, but it has a slight positive effect when the wife's attainment is not greater. For the wife, the effect of the husband's perception of balance is stronger when her attainment surpasses her husband's. This finding makes sense; when the wife's attainment is less than her husband's and when he still regards the relationship as balanced, that situation has a positive effect on him. When her attainment surpasses his and when he is still unthreatened, that situation has a positive effect on her.

It is interesting to see that the husband's support for his wife's working has a positive effect on each partner's perceived marital quality only when her attainment is not greater than his. Among couples in which the wife's attainment surpasses the husband's, that support is related negatively to marital quality. There appears to be a difference between support for the wife's working and support for her achieving.

SUMMARY

This chapter has focused on the importance of competitiveness, balance, gender-role identity, and support for the marital quality described by husbands and by wives. We have examined more closely how those relationships are altered by the wife's participation in the labor force and by her achievement relative to her husband's.

The husband's competitiveness, as demonstrated by his need to surpass his wife, has negative consequences for both spouses' marital quality in almost all situations. The only exception occurs when the wife participates in the labor force but when her achievement is less than her husband's. Even then the effect is neutral only for the wife.

The wife's need to be better than her husband also has negative effects on marital quality, especially for her. Those effects are even more negative when she participates in the labor force and when her achievement is less than her husband's.

The negative influence of competitiveness on marriage may have been underestimated in the past. The functionalists, who foresaw the negative consequences of competition, believed that those effects could be avoided if the wife stayed out of the labor force or participated in a job that conferred less status than her husband's. (This suggestion implies that only the husband, not the wife, would have a competitive attitude.) The findings in this study suggest that the negative effects of a husband's need to surpass his wife are almost universal. The negative effects of the wife's competitiveness appear to be avoided when she does not participate in the labor force but are stronger if she does participate in the labor force and achieves less than her husband. The simple conclusion most consistent with these data is that one partner's need to be better than his or her spouse is incompatible with the emotional bonds that produce high-quality marriages.

The perception of balance also is related to marital quality. The wife experiences more positive marital quality if her husband perceives their relationship as more balanced, especially when she participates in the labor force and when her achievement surpasses her husband's. In a dual-earner marriage a husband who perceives the relationship as unbalanced may feel dependent on his wife, who earns income as well as providing most of the housekeeping and child care. These feelings of dependency can be the basis of conflict in a marriage. Men who do not feel threatened by their wives' achievements appear to provide a stronger basis for high-quality marriages.

The effects of the wife's perception of balance are not as great as those of the husband's. If she is more successful than her husband in the labor force, however, her marital quality is substantially lower insofar as she perceives the situation to be more unbalanced. In this event she may feel that her husband is not contributing his fair share. As we saw in the last chapter, few men participate in housekeeping; the majority perform less than half of the child care tasks. If a wife is the main provider and at the same time must take care of the house and the children, she is likely to develop at least some resentment.

The single most important finding about gender-role is the pervasive importance of husband's sensitivity. Regardless of the wife's participation in the labor force or her relative achievement, a husband with a supportive personality, sensitive to his wife's feelings, is critical in a high-quality marriage. His assertiveness is largely irrelevant, and his wife's predominant trait cluster is not critical; his sensitivity is what matters.

The husband's support for his wife's working and her perception of his attitude affects marital quality in predictable ways. If the husband supports his wife's participation in the labor force and if she does work, marital quality is increased; if she does not work, the quality of their marriage is lower. Support for the wife's working, however, is not the same as support for her achieving. Many couples in which the husband supports the wife's working experience lower marital quality when the wife's achievement is greater than her husband's.

If a single conclusion underlies these findings, it is the importance of the husband's sensitivity. In the better marriages for both husbands and wives, the husband is sensitive and supportive, does not need to be better than his wife, and is not threatened by her achievements.

CHAPTER SEVEN

Successful Marriages

We have described social changes that affect the structure and functioning of the family, and in particular we have noted two relatively new developments: the widespread employment of women outside the home and the relative instability of modern marriage. That men and women can survive economically as individuals, independent of one another, is truly a new circumstance. In the long view, there is evidence of growing sex equality in modern society, and we have focused on the meaning of this trend for marriage. In this book we have asked: What does this potential for independence mean for the institution of marriage? What is the difference between dual-earner marriages and traditional single-earner marriages? Why are women with graduate degrees and/or above-average personal incomes four times as likely to divorce as women with lower occupational achievements?

We assume an important link between immediate social circumstances and the view of self, between the structure of social behavior and modal personality characteristics. The slow but definite evolution from patriarchal forms toward sex equality places the focus on individuals' gender roles and gender-role identities. In this research we asked whether individuals' perceptions, attitudes, and psychological propensities with respect to gender-related concerns account significantly for the marital quality perceived by women and by men in both single- and dual-earner marriages. The answer is yes.

In fact, the answer is pointed. Our results suggest that at this time the onus is on the husbands. Our concise but unsatisfactory advice to women pursuing occupational success and marital success is to marry wisely. The most important elements in the quality of all marriages, especially those with working and high-achieving wives, are the husband's sensitivity, supportiveness, and sense of self-worth. Of course this finding does not excuse wives from sharing the responsibility for marital quality; marital success always will require the positive contribution of two individuals. Our findings, however, reflect our situation as a society undergoing social change, and, thus, they are not surprising.

Historically, the structural power in society has belonged to men. Some people would point out—correctly—that as a total society, we are far from achieving equality between women and men. Yet circumstances are changing so that women have an increasing share of the power to make decisions and command resources. Women's roles in the social system have changed more than men's. Women have been pulled rapidly into the labor force, but they have not relinquished domestic and child-care responsibilities or shared them with men at a similar rate. Women also have been socialized to serve, support, and care for the men in their lives. From an individual perspective the change in women's labor-force participation over the last 25 years "just happened"; it was not intended or contrived but occurred through the decisions of many individual couples.

Although some women have found the change painful (many would not have chosen it), they are in a new position today. In the long run, that position is advantageous to them, and they are experiencing it as such. Opportunities to be self-supporting (although mostly at lower income levels) have brought the rewards of self-reliance, self-confidence, freedom, and growth. Although, in general, women are still highly motivated caregivers and find much of their identity in nurturing children, spouses, parents, friends, and neighbors, they may be less likely today to be blind to their own needs, to play martyr or victim, or to allow themselves to be exploited in personal relationships. On the one hand, traditional gender-role socialization for women has generated a sensitive, supportive, pleasing approach to interpersonal relations. On the other hand, the new circumstances have sensitized women to inequities, to the personal power and self-determination that they lacked in the past, and to occasions when they were not treated with dignity in close or secondary relationships.

Men also find themselves in curious new circumstances. In contrast to women, men may believe that the direction of change involves loss rather than gain of status. They would not embrace such a change if they perceived it in this way, but would be more likely to avoid or ignore it. In addition, traditional socialization patterns provide little training for the behaviors now expected of men. Having been taught to compete, to be aggressive, to hide weakness, men find modern expectations confusing. To be manly has meant, above all, not to be womanly, but success in close relationships now appears to require acknowledging and expressing the traditionally feminine traits of sensitivity and supportiveness. In successful contemporary marriages between economically independent women and men, husbands have been able to let go the *more than* image of maleness and to support their partners and their partners' achievements. In this chapter we summarize the line of thought behind our research, point out the overall findings, and draw some conclusions about the present and the future.

SUMMARY

Because women's and men's social roles and their relative status and power are changing, although slowly, it is not surprising that the requirements of stable and successful marriages also may change. Gender roles and husband's and wife's roles are related closely and overlap for many people; these roles or societal prescriptions are internalized by individuals to varying degrees. Women and men incorporate the typically masculine or feminine role expectations of assertiveness and sensitivity into their own self-concepts in significantly different ways. We refer to what is internalized—what is taken as part of the self—as one's gender-role identity.

Individuals can change and can adapt their role identities to new circumstances. Some attitudes, however, are likely to be maintained forcefully and consistently through one's life; a deep awareness of self and a concerted conscious effort may be required to modify them. Perhaps it is more likely that widespread change will occur over large groups or generations of people rather than in individual lives.

Social Change

In over half of today's intact marriages both spouses are employed, and projections suggest that women's and men's employment rates will become very similar within the next few decades. Divorce data suggest the stress and strain of maintaining dual-earner marriages; the most highly educated and best-paid women are at greatest risk of their marriages being dissolved.

Changes in the scale of human society have created structural and functional changes in organization that demand qualitative changes in human relationships. Increasing specialization and differentiation are the basis for a process of social individuation, making the individual rather than the group the focus of human activity. Ogburn (1966 [1922]) identified the problems inherent in cultural lag; many identifiable social problems and individual neuroses are likely to result when one part of a sociocultural system is not in equilibrium with another. At the present time there may be a lack of adjustment between the changing characteristics of the social structure, related to declining sex stratification and to women's and men's behaviors and attitudes within marriage.

Women always have participated in economic production, but for most of human history they were able to do so in or near the home, where they could combine that activity with housekeeping and child care. Now nearly all economic production occurs outside the home. Women are participating in great numbers, and consequently our society is struggling with the development of effective strategies for housekeeping and good quality child care. Social institutions, including the family, have experienced shifting functions and responsibilities.

The sources of social change include dramatic demographic, technological, and economic developments. After the Industrial Revolution, human reproduction became far more efficient; fewer births were required to produce a comparable number of productive adults. This change has brought profound freedom to women's lives. Technological innovations were responsible for dispersing many functions that the family had fulfilled in agrarian society to different institutions in industrial society. Modern society is organized occupationally; one's work defines a specific functional task and provides one with a definite social position and status. The occupational structure contains a high degree of sex segregation, but this structure is in flux. The constantly changing division of labor alters work roles and will continue to affect women's and men's relative status.

These changes in our material life have stimulated changes in our perspective on the world, our values, and our beliefs. People in American society place a high premium on individual liberty, creativity, and responsibility. If women are to share in the same rights and obligations as men, family forms must be revised so that women are no more and no less constrained than men by taking care of the young and the old. It is unlikely, however, that nurturing activities will receive their proper due until men, as well as women, cultivate the abilities to perform them and share in their delivery. The new individualism, autonomy, and independence must be matched by an equal measure of human attachment, connectedness, and intimacy if families and societies are to function effectively. Social relationships may develop more slowly than the economic relationships that dominate them, but eventually they must become appropriate to the conditions of obtaining sustenance. Regaining that equilibrium may require modification in individual roles and identities.

Changing Roles and Identities

Individual selves are products of their particular experience in society. Individuals' new, creative approaches to their social roles also reshape social structure, slowly but steadily. Gender is a typically salient element of one's identity; gender roles describe culturally constructed clusters of characteristics regarded as typical or appropriate for males or females in a specific society. In contrast to sex, which is innate or ascribed, gender roles are learned and achieved. These roles are pervasive because they represent a system of stratification embedded in society rather than having reference only to a more limited group. Spousal and parental roles are so ubiquitous and so sex-specific that they are identified closely with gender roles.

Through the socialization process known as sex-typing, individuals incorporate some pattern of traditionally masculine or feminine behaviors into their own sense of self; the result is gender-role identity. Although some propensities certainly develop early in life, typical masculine and feminine characteristics, assertiveness and sensitivity respectively, are normative behaviors and attitudes, reinforced continually through social interaction with significant others. When an individual finds role performances especially fulfilling, the associated characteristics become part of his or her sense of self. Yet social interaction is fluid and changing precisely because people vary their role performances.

In the mid-twentieth century, psychologists typically saw conformity to typical gender roles as appropriate and healthy. More recently, theorists have pointed out the ways in which this conformity is difficult for many individuals. They conclude that perhaps the lack of fit exists between the gender-role stereotypes and the objective social environment rather than between the stereotypes and individuals. Some psychologists have noted the desirability of acknowledging, integrating, and using both assertiveness and sensitivity within oneself, and recent literature has used the term androgyny to describe this ability or tendency.

Much of what we have learned suggests that some present-day marital difficulty is attributable to people's attachment to earlier social roles. Circumstances seem to demand that both women and men let go some of those expectations and interact with more flexibility. Marriage involves roles, but potentially it is also the most intimate of all relationships. The nature of such a relationship is that individuals interact as whole selves, exposing their feelings, beliefs, and values. Being in touch with one's personal identity and sharing one's uniqueness openly with an intimate partner are essential to successful egalitarian marriages; strongly reinforced gender roles may interfere with this kind of interaction. Identity, intimacy, marriage, and growth are tied together inextricably in the life process. If a person does not disclose a true self, it cannot be validated by the reaction of others. The traditional gender-role definitions and modes of relating in marriage may serve more to maintain the status quo than to foster individual growth.

The Thesis

We believe that significant social and economic forces have changed human life in ways that urge women and men to adopt different self-concepts and behaviors in order to sustain high-quality marriages. Human personality and the social world are one interdependent system. At the broad social level, marital discord and divorce have resulted from external social circumstances that provide individuals with opportunities for greater flexibility and freedom. If marriages are to endure, both more flexibility and more responsibility are required on the part of individuals.

Now women as well as men are being affected by the social individuation that accompanied the Industrial Revolution and by the ideology of individualism that developed at the same time. As women have been drawn into the labor force, their roles, like those of men, have become more achieved than ascribed. It is possible that the late twentieth century is witnessing the dawn of a more substantial sex equality; that equality necessarily will exist in intimate man-woman relationships as well as in the wider society. If this is so, marriages will be different from those of the past. Because stability is no longer to be assumed on the basis of the economic structure, a stable marriage also must be achieved rather than ascribed.

In our research we studied 489 married couples, some in single-earner marriages and some in dual-earner marriages, including a number of couples in which the wives' occupational achievements equaled or surpassed those of their husbands. We asked partners to describe their own self-concepts with respect to typical gender-associated traits. We also asked them about three other attitudes that seem to be interwoven closely with gender-role concerns and consciousness: their marital role expectations and their perceptions of partner's expectations, their sense of balance or complementarity of marital role behaviors, and their own sense of competitiveness.

The literature contains theories about all four of these phenomena as social psychological determinants of marital stress or marital quality. We were interested in the comparative power of the explanations for success in marriage, in the additional effects of wife's employment, and particularly in the additional effects of the wife's occupational achievements relative to her husband's. The dependent variable was a measure of perceived marital quality; the section that follows describes our findings.

Findings

Marital Quality

Most of the couples in our sample perceive the events of their marriages in fairly neutral terms but feel satisfied with what they have. More than 90% stated they quarreled with their spouse or that he or she got on their nerves, but more than 85% hardly ever or never regretted marrying that person. Husbands and wives appear to perceive the quality of marriages in much the same way; we found no consistent differences between them.

Socioeconomic variables had no effect on the quality of marriage experienced by spouses. Neither the levels of family income, husband's occupational status, husband's education, nor wife's education had any effect. We found no direct effect for whether or not the wife was employed or for whether she surpassed her husband's achievements. It seems fundamental, and perhaps comforting, that the perceived quality of the marital relationship is immune (at least directly) from these socioeconomic differences.

In a 1983 study using a national sample, we found that women employed in a nontraditional occupation (one held normally by men) were more likely than other women to experience negative marital and/or career changes during a seven-year period. In this sample we found that wife's employment in a traditional or nontraditional occupation did not affect the quality of marriage as perceived by husbands but that it did make a difference for wives. Women employed in male sex-typed jobs experienced lower-quality marriages; such jobs may create certain pressures or may cause a direct comparison with husbands that is not found in other occupational circumstances.

The stages of the life cycle influence the quality of marriage experienced, but only mildly. Although the number of children does not have an effect, couples with children at home perceive lower marital quality than those without children at home. Children demand much of their parents' attention and energy, which partners otherwise might direct toward each other, and probably they also contribute to conflictive situations and frustrations for their parents.

Both husbands and wives in marriages of less than 5 years' duration experience higher marital quality than those in marriages of between 5 and 10 years. Curiously, husbands married more than 10 years perceive a quality comparable to that of the first 5 years, while wives do not. Wives married more than 10 years perceive a lower quality of marriage, more comparable to that of the second 5-year period.

The older husbands are, the higher the quality of marriage they perceive. The opposite is true for wives, although the relationship is not as strong. This finding may be the result of the role transitions of our times.

Role Expectations and Performances

In many marriages today, couples must negotiate a household division of labor that once was a given. Two jobs in one family, particularly if children are present, inevitably create an overload of work and detail that does not exist in one-job families. These demands in themselves create the possibility of dissension. We posited that marital quality would be enhanced by a match between the role expectations and the performances of self and of partner.

Nearly all wives and husbands expect both partners to share in child care; most respondents also believe that money management should be a shared responsibility. In contrast, half believe that housework is the wife's responsibility and over half believe that earning income is the husband's. When we examined what these couples perceive as the actual division of labor in their marriages, we discovered that only one-third of the husbands perform any regular household task, and only half help with child-care tasks. Obviously, many people are living with a mismatch between expectations and realities. In general, the role expectations of both husbands and wives are less traditional when the wife is employed, but role expectations and performances do not vary with differences in other socioeconomic or life cycle variables.

Our findings have significant implications for the quality of marriage. Both husbands and wives report better marriages when the wife's role expectations are more traditional and when she perceives her husband's role expectations as less traditional. It is also important that the wife's employment match the husband's expectations. When the wife is not in the labor force, partners experience higher marital quality if the husband's expectations are more traditional. When the wife is in the labor force, partners experience higher marital quality if the husband's expectations are less traditional. Yet whether or not the wife is in the labor force, and regardless of what the husband actually believes, wives perceive their own marital quality as lower when they perceive their husbands' expectations as more traditional. Women are willing to live traditionally, but apparently do not appreciate being expected to do so.

Partners generally agree about who does what around the house. Perceptions of what the spouse expects also are important, and errors in perceptions occur. Often husbands are less traditional and wives are more traditional than their spouses believe them to be. This finding suggests that more and better communication could be significant in increasing the marital quality experienced by spouses.

Competitiveness, Balance, and Gender-Role Identity

As we expected, competitiveness causes problems that have implications for spouses' marital quality. If the wife feels competitive with her spouse, her marital quality suffers, especially when she is in the labor force and is achieving less occupationally than her husband. If the husband feels competitive with his spouse, both partners experience less marital quality in all employment status situations but one: when the wife is in the labor force and is achieving less than her husband. In this case, his competitiveness does not affect her marital quality, but it still affects his.

Years ago the Parsonian theorists argued that if women stayed out of the labor force, achievement comparisons and competition between spouses would be avoided. Our data suggest that if those feelings exist, they have negative influences on the relationship whether or not the wife works. It may be true, however, that equal achievements on her part might exacerbate the situation.

Role complementarity or balance in the relationship is a factor in marital quality, but it is a less powerful predictor than the other explanatory models. The more balance the husband perceives in role behaviors, the higher the wife's perceived marital quality, especially when she is in the labor force and especially when her achievements equal or surpass her husband's. Wives apparently are aware of their husbands' sense of security in this respect; if a husband is comfortable with the degree of role complementarity and is not threatened by his wife's achievements, the wife's marital quality is enhanced.

The wife's perception of balance is less significant except when her achievements are equal to or greater than her husband's and when she perceives an imbalance. In such a case her own sense of marital quality suffers.

The effects of gender-role identity on both spouses' marital quality are clear and strong. The wife's gender-role identity is not critical in any employment condition, though her own marital quality is enhanced slightly when her sensitivity is stronger; her husband's marital quality is enhanced slightly when her assertiveness is weaker. Neither is the degree of the husband's assertiveness important for the partners' marital quality. It has no effect for either spouse.

By far the most critical factor is the husband's sensitivity, the degree of supportiveness that he can display. This is the strongest and most significant finding in the study. Marital quality for both spouses depends on a husband's ability to provide the emotional support that deepens the attachment in the marital bond, whether or not the wife is in the labor force and whether or not she exhibits high occupational achievements. Apparently a husband who acknowledges and exhibits the supportive elements of his personality creates a positive situation. Receiving that support improves the quality of the wife's marriage; giving that support improves the quality of the husband's. This finding is completely consistent with the theory that more flexible gender-role identities are congruent with stable marriages today.

CONCLUSIONS

The research literature on marriage shows that couples in which wives have high occupational achievements are at greater risk for marital stress and dissolution. Wife's employment alone does not have such effects. Most women work; most husbands expect wives to work and appreciate the additional income. In the segregated labor force, however, most wives work at jobs not comparable in status and income to those held by men. Some couples whose occupational achievements are comparable are successful in their marriages. We wished to discover something about the secret of their success. In our data we found that the life cycle has effects on the marital quality experienced. These effects are the same as those found by other researchers; they represent the fluctuations in satisfaction that all people experience over the years. We found that the direct effects of differences in socioeconomic status, no matter what variables we used in measurement, were not important in predicting marital quality. The spouses' attitudes and perceptions about themselves and their partners are more powerful explanations for stress or success in relationships.

Toward Marital Success

Each of the theoretical models tested here shows explanatory value, and relationships are in the direction predicted. Some lessons can be learned, then, for the achievement of marital quality. The first is that role expectations, whatever they are, need to be discussed. Some couples may have different expectations; they must negotiate and reach an understanding about how they will manage their family. Many couples, however, may have more similar expectations than they perceive individually. Partners' perceptions about their spouses' feelings, often unverified, have a powerful influence on their own comfort in the relationship, and often they are in error. The key appears to be that both partners express honest feelings and find the compromises that work for them. It is also possible that the more couples communicate, the more they may come to share a similar outlook.

The second piece of advice offered by this study is that feelings of competition have no legitimate place in a marriage. Competition may be useful in other situations in more distant, secondary relationships, but the marital bond requires consistent mutual support and encouragement. Competition is the antithesis of support; it may add stimulation in play, but it cannot be serious or concern matters important to individual identities. Latent feelings of competition with one's partner must be acknowledged and addressed by the individual.

The third general finding is that the perceived balance of costs and rewards in a marriage is relevant to success. This felt or perceived balance, the element of equity, matters more than any objective reality. We found that when high-achieving women (who still are likely to be carrying more than half the domestic responsibilities) feel an imbalance, their marital quality suffers. It is possible that couples keep a mental ledger on the equity of costs and rewards, and probably there is some range beyond which the imbalance becomes intolerable to one or the other.

An interesting point in our findings is that the husband's sense of equity improves the quality of marriage for the wife. It is his view that matters; if he is comfortable, apparently she is aware of it and her sense of the relationship is enhanced. This element is more important for employed wives and even more so for high-achieving wives. A husband's support for his wife's breadwinning capacity also is likely to reflect comfort with himself. Husbands who can communicate "I'm OK and you're OK" give significant support to their wives, particularly in circumstances in which the wives feel deviant, such as when they are high occupational achievers.

It is understandable why the wife's perception of balance is less influential in the same way. Although she may well feel and communicate "I'm OK and you're OK" in a marriage in which she is the higher achiever, the societal pressures are greater on males to achieve than on females not to achieve.

The fourth lesson is that flexibility in gender-role expectations, particularly on the part of husbands, can contribute significantly to marital quality. Our direct measure of how partners see themselves—their own self-concepts—with respect to gender-linked traits was important. The husbands' self-concepts were far more important than those of wives. Husbands who identified themselves as more sensitive and more supportive experienced better marriages, and so did their wives.

Overall, the degree of spouses' assertiveness (instrumental and leadership behavior) was not very significant for the relationship. In contrast, the degree of sensitivity (empathetic and supportive behavior) was significant. Perhaps this finding should not be surprising; if people are sufficiently instrumental to cope with life, lack of instrumentality should not be a problem in a close relationship. A partner's understanding, empathy, and support are likely to be more critical.

There appears to be no substitute for this kind of giving in a marriage. Without one partner's economic dependence, the giving must take place in two directions. Contemporary marriages, which no longer fit the traditional sex stratification, challenge us to the core of our personalities. If such marriages are to be successful, husbands must rid themselves of the need to feel "more than" and wives must let go of needing to feel "less than" their partners in the traditional ways. Today it is more necessary that partners be friends and companions, able to communicate openly with one another.

The Future

What might we expect for marriages in the future? Certainly this research and this discussion contain an implicit value judgment: people should experience well-being and satisfaction in their close relationships. Insofar as this occurs, those relationships will be stable. The world changes, however; people grow and change, and a stable marriage does not mean a static marriage. The relationship must live too. Partners will be called on increasingly to maximize flexibility and to invest effort in their relationship if it is to survive. To the extent that stability in marriage supports individual well-being, it is functional for society; individuals supported sufficiently by significant others are more likely to be healthy and productive. In addition to providing emotional gratification for members, the other remaining significant function of families is rearing children. Stable, loving relationships are important to this process, and strong marriages make a contribution.

In view of individual economic freedom and the present high level of expectations with respect to fulfillment in marriage, the most rational prediction may be an increase in the rates of divorce and serial marriage. People now are free from past structure and from the normative constraints that necessitated either trying harder and making marriages better or resigning themselves to what they had. They are living longer, and change in the world is occurring faster. How likely is it that partners can grow and change in ways sufficiently compatible to maintain their relationships? Both women and men are demanding more of their partners. Will it become apparent that they must also demand more of themselves?

Prediction is risky; the institution of marriage will change as society itself evolves. The societal pressures toward sex equality are modifying the basic man-woman union. Wives' and husbands' roles are changing as new situations and new opportunities arise; overall, the status of marital relationships is likely to be turbulent for some time. Even so, we may be on the brink of a new awareness of our own human needs and a new acceptance of responsibility for providing for them. Successful egalitarian marriages are made by individuals who know and accept themselves and who feel free to be themselves. These partners work out their own destinies alone and together, with autonomy and passion. The exercise of power as the expression of dominance and submission is not a part of these interpersonal relationships. The key is love, expressed as an authentic acceptance of and interest in one's own developing identity and in that of one's partner.

Because human beings attach themselves to one another and because marriage offers one of the major opportunities for personal growth, it is unlikely ever to be taken lightly. Our emerging identities develop through the frustrations and satisfactions of confronting ourselves daily through another human being. It may be that we will increase our abilities to look at, accept, and expose ourselves and to communicate with our partners.

Divorce always will be a safety valve for those who make wrong choices at the beginning, or for couples in which partners grow on different time schedules. Yet it may become a less-used option among those who see the process itself, the striving for marital success, as a clear route to ultimate fulfillment in life. The tide in human affairs, as reflected in the social and psychological levels of analysis, suggests this possibility.

In reviewing recent centuries of family change, Gadlin (1977) describes the expansion of personal consciousness that accompanies modernization. As he notes, intimacy in relationships accompanies the individualism that social differentiation provided. Such intimacy assumes sincere emotional equality. This kind of relationship inevitably will be supported by partners who are peers in achievements, responsibilities, and the ability to care for one another.

APPENDIX

The Work and Family Study Sample

DATA COLLECTION

The data for the Work and Family Study were collected between October 1982 and March 1983. The initial study plan called for personal interviews with a sample of 450 couples in the Cincinnati, Ohio metropolitan area (Hamilton County), consisting of 300 dual-earner couples and 150 couples in which only the husband was employed. These kinds of couples exist in approximately equal numbers in the population, but we oversampled this category because dual-earner couples were to be the focus of the study. The study was concerned with relative occupational statuses of spouses, so it was important to include a sufficient number of women whose occupational status might surpass their husbands'. We decided to oversample women in professional and managerial occupations sex-typed as male so that at least 50 couples would be in this category and so would provide a sufficient number for analysis.

This stratified sample was drawn as callers dialed random numbers and screened subjects. In the beginning, any married couple in which the husband was employed was eligible. As data collection proceeded and after 150 husband-only-employed couples had been selected, we reclassified only dual-earner couples as eligible. Toward the end, when we had selected 250 couples with wives in occupations other than professional/managerial occupations sex-typed as male, only couples in these occupations remained eligible. These occupations belong to the professional and managerial census categories in which 60% or more of the occupants are male. In the analyses, we weighted numbers in terms of the actual proportions of wives employed and of wives employed in those occupations in Hamilton County.

Both men and women callers screened households between six and nine o'clock on weeknights and on Saturdays; interviews were scheduled at the subjects' convenience. Addresses were sought from eligible couples who hesitated to make interview appointments, and information about the study was mailed. This letter was followed by a callback and, if necessary, by a second letter and callback. Those who refused to give addresses or who refused initially to answer the screening questions also were called a second time. Hesitant potential subjects also were given a phone number to verify the authenticity of the study; approximately 10 subjects called the number, and most of these ultimately participated. In summary, 27.6% of eligible households accepted immediately, 15.8% after a first letter, 2.3% after a second letter, and 1.6% after a callback with no information sent.

MODIFICATION OF SAMPLE

Halfway through the data collection process it became apparent that we could secure a reasonable number of interviews from couples in which only the wife was employed. (The national economy during this period was plagued with high unemployment.) Considering the subject matter of the study, we decided that it would be useful to interview as many of the wife-only-employed couples as we knew were available in our sample of households. Eighty-six such couples were identified in the screening of households; we sought funds to interview as many as 50 of these couples, and we completed interviews with 39 (45.3%).

RESPONSE RATE

Including the wife-only-employed couples, eligible households numbered 1037; 489 interviews were completed. The acceptance rate (the percentage of couples contacted who agreed to be interviewed) was 47%. The preferred report of sample coverage, however, is the response rate, which is the percentage of all eligible subjects in the population who are included in the sample. In this case, among the 369 households called at which we received a busy signal, no answer, or a refusal of screen, we cannot be sure how many belonged in the eligible category. If the 21.7% of the working numbers identified as eligible households can be considered an adequate guide, another 80 households might have been eligible, making an estimated response rate of 43.8% (489/(1037+80)).

SAMPLE DISTRIBUTIONS ON SELECTED VARIABLES

Tables A.1 and A.2 present the distribution of the sample on employment, family, and income data respectively. Ninety-two percent of husbands and 70% of wives were employed. Sixty-two percent of the husbands liked the fact that their wives were in the labor force or wished they were. Over 30% of husbands viewed lack of time for each other as the major problem of having two jobs in one family, while 30% of the wives viewed completing household tasks as the major problem.

The sample represented all ages; over 7% of the couples were other than white. Nearly all subjects had some education or training beyond high school. All but one-fifth had at least one child, and of those who had children, 85% still had at least one child at home. Average family income of the sample was

Table A.1 Employment, Employment Attitudes, and Income of Spouses

Employment	Husbands		Wives	
	N	%	N	%
Employed	452	92.4	345	70.6
Umemployed (looking)	16	3.3	17	3.5
Not in labor force	21	4.3	127	26.0

Attitude toward Wife's Employment (Husbands)
Perceived Attitude of Husband (Wives)

	Husbands		Wives	
	N	%	N	%
Likes very much	179	36.6	200	40.9
Likes somewhat	126	25.8	130	26.6
Doesn't care	74	15.1	79	16.2
Dislikes somewhat	76	15.5	55	11.2
Dislikes very much	27	5.5	25	5.1

The Major Problem of Two Jobs in One Marriage

	Husbands		Wives	
	N	%	N	%
Time for each other	160	32.7	131	26.8
Child care	93	19.0	80	16.4
Doing household tasks	83	17.0	149	30.5
Time for self	5	1.0	7	1.4
Coordinating things	27	5.5	26	5.3
Lack of energy	21	4.3	22	4.5
No problems	47	9.6	31	6.3
Other	34	7.0	29	5.9

Income	Husbands		Wives		Family	
	N	%	N	%	N	%
0–9,999	14	2.9	80	16.4	4	0.8
10,000–19,999	119	24.3	162	33.1	47	9.6
20,000–29,999	143	29.2	66	13.5	94	19.2
30,000–39,999	91	18.6	16	3.3	33	27.2
40,000–49,999	29	5.3	2	.4	89	18.2
50,000–59,999	16	3.3	0	.0	41	8.4
60,000–69,000	26	5.3	3	.6	62	12.7
Missing	51	10.4	160	32.7	19	3.9

Table A.2 Demographic Family Variables

Race	Husbands		Wives		Number of Children		
	N	%	N	%	#	N	%
White	451	92.2	453	92.6	0	97	19.8
Black	33	6.7	32	6.5	1	78	16.0
Other	3	0.6	4	0.8	2	137	28.0
					3	84	17.2
					4	41	8.4
					5	26	5.3
					6+	23	4.6

Age	Husbands		Wives		Of Those Who Have Children, Number Still at Home		
	N	%	N	%	#	N	%
20–29	111	22.7	149	30.5	0	72	14.7
30–39	151	30.9	150	30.8	1	117	23.9
40–49	91	18.6	84	15.4	2	138	28.2
50–59	101	20.6	86	17.6	3	52	10.6
60+	35	7.2	20	1.6	4	17	3.5
					5	7	1.4
					6+	3	0.6

Years of Education	Husbands		Wives	
	N	%	N	%
11 or less	0	0.0	2	.4
12	13	2.7	15	3.1
13	12	2.5	23	4.7
14	27	5.5	8	1.6
15	25	5.1	19	3.9
16	30	6.1	30	6.1
17	26	5.3	26	5.3
18	27	5.5	24	4.9
19	16	3.3	2	.4
20+	21	7.1	7	1.4

considerably above the average for the population; the median was $38,260. Most of these couples, of course, were two-income families.

Because the response rate was not as high as we would have liked, we compared information for the sample with information gathered by questionnaire from as many people as possible among those who refused to be interviewed, and also with parallel information from the 1980 census.

INFORMATION FROM NONPARTICIPANTS

Although people may not be willing to participate in a survey, they may consent to provide some information in another form. While scheduling interviews, 266 of the couples who refused ultimately to participate had given their names and addresses. We located 170 additional addresses of couples who had not given their identities, using two city directories. We mailed a two-page questionnaire with a stamped return envelope to these 436 couples, asking some of the demographic and other questions central to the study, as well as why they had refused to participate; 162 (37%) returned the questionnaire. Consequently some key information is available for 30% of the 548 refusals or for another 16% of the sample, hence for 63% of the total sample drawn.

When we compared the demographic information received from nonparticipants via questionnaires with information from participants in the study, we found that it conformed closely to findings of earlier studies (Hawkins, 1975). As Table A.3 shows, the participants are of higher socioeconomic status and are younger than the nonparticipants. It appears that more of the participants were employed in professional and managerial positions, had about one more year of education on the average, earned about $2000 a year more, and were four or five years younger. Unfortunately, these differences probably understate the bias in the sample, because many couples neither participated in the survey nor returned questionnaires.

Table A.3 Mean and Proportion Comparisons of Nonparticipants with Participants

Variables	Nonparticipants N = 162	Participants N = 489
Husband's occupation		
Professional-managerial	36%	44%
Clerical-sales	24%	20%
Service	5%	4%
Skilled, semiskilled, unskilled labor	35%	32%
Percentage wives employed	67%	71%
Wife's occupation		
Professional-managerial	29%	42%
Clerical-sales	53%	43%
Service	9%	9%
Skilled, semiskilled, unskilled labor	8%	6%
Husband's education	13.7	14.8
Wife's education	12.9	13.9
Husband's earnings	$26,664	$28,141
Wife's earnings	$13,644	$15,430
Husband's age	45.4	40.4
Wife's age	42.5	38.0
Percentage white	91%	93%
Number of children living at home	1.5	1.6
Husband's comparison of job status	2.9	2.5
Wife's comparison of job status	1.7	1.7
Husband's comparison of job success	2.4	2.3
Wife's comparison of job success	1.9	1.9
Husband's marital satisfaction	0.7	0.6
Wife's marital satisfaction	0.9	0.7
Husband's marital regret	3.5	3.5
Wife's marital regret	3.3	3.4

The greatest advantage of the nonparticipant questionnaire is the opportunity to compare information on some nondemographic information, because better demographic information may be available from other sources. Both participants in the survey and people who received the nonparticipant questionnaires were questioned about their marital satisfaction and about their occupational status and success relative to their spouses'. Responses to these questions are virtually identical for both groups. Although the sample certainly is biased demographically, the demographic variables may not be related to the variables of key interest in the study; therefore, the latter may conform more closely to the unknown population distribution.

When asked why they did not participate in the survey, about half of those couples who returned the nonparticipant questionnaire said that they did not have the time. The next most frequent responses were "desire for privacy" and "just unwilling." In many cases we learned that only one of the spouses in the couple was unwilling.

INFORMATION FROM THE CENSUS

The sampling area of the survey conformed to a reporting area of the census, so it was possible to obtain an estimate of bias in the sample by comparing results of the survey with the census. In this case the participants in the survey were compared with similar persons reported in the 1980 Bureau of the Census 5% sample of Hamilton County, Ohio, found in the public-user data. Information from the census was limited to married couples with at least one spouse employed. The sample of participants was weighted by both spouses' labor-force participation and by the wife's employment in male-dominated professional or managerial occupations. We carried out the weighting because the sample had been stratified initially on these variables. Comparisons between the sample and the census are presented in Table A.4.

The comparisons between the 1980 census and the sample of married couples show that participants in the sample are of higher socioeconomic status, especially with respect to income. Family income differs by approximately $10,000 because both higher-earning husbands and higher-earning wives participated in the survey. Some (but not all) of the difference is attributable to inflation between 1980 and 1983. In connection with socioeconomic status, participants in the survey take longer to get to work, perhaps because they live in residential areas farther from areas of business and industry. They also are more likely to be

Table A.4 Mean and Proportion Comparisons of 1980 Census with Sample

Variable	1980 Census N = 3,908	Weighted Sample N = 489
Family income	$28,711	$38,260
Husband's wages (both working)	$18,200	$25,690
Wife's wages (both working)	$7,805	$15,729
Husband's education	14.17	14.82
Wife's education	13.54	13.73
Wife's number of children	3.26	2.32
Husband's age	42.95	40.93
Wife's age	40.45	38.57
Husband's minutes to work	10.57	20.90
Wife's minutes to work	5.09	18.47
Husbands' percentage white	87.4%	93.0%
Wives' percentage white	87.8%	93.0%
Husbands' percentage first marriages	83.8%	83.0%
Wives' percentage first marriages	85.1%	83.0%

white and to have fewer children. Wife's education was the only socioeconomic variable for which the difference between the sample and the census was not significant at the .05 level, and it was nearly significant.

Number of marriages was the only other comparison variable for which a difference was not found. Approximately equal percentages of individuals, both husbands and wives, were in their first marriage. Demographic variables may be sensitive to response rates, but marital variables seem to be less so.

References

Abrahams, Barbara, S., Feldman, Shirley, and Nash, Sharon Churnin (1978) Sex role self-concept and sex role attitudes: Enduring personality characteristics or adaptations to changing life situations? *Developmental Psychology, 14*, 393–400.

Axelson, Leland J. (1963) The marital adjustment and marital role definitions of husbands of working and nonworking wives. *Marriage and Family Living, 24*, 189–195.

Bahr, Stephen J., Chappell, C. Bradford, and Leigh, Geoffrey K. (1983) Age at marriage, role enactment, role consensus and marital satisfaction. *Journal of Marriage and the Family, 45*, 795–803.

Bakan, David (1966) *The duality of human existence.* Chicago: Rand McNally.

Barber, Bernard (1956) *Social stratification: A comparative analysis of structure and process.* New York: Harcourt Brace.

Becker, Gary S. (1973) A theory of marriage: Part I. *Journal of Political Economy, 81*, 813–846.

Becker, Gary S., Kanes, E. M., and Michael, R. T. (1977) An economic analysis of marital instability. *Journal of Political Economy, 85*, 1141–1187.

Bem, Sandra L. (1974) The measurement of psychological androgyny. *Journal of Consulting and Clinical Psychology, 42*, 155–162.

———(1975) Sex-role adaptability: One consequence of psychological androgyny. *Journal of Personality and Social Psychology, 31*, 634–643.

———(1981a) Gender schema theory: A cognitive account of sex-typing. *Psychological Review, 88*, 354–364.

———(1981b) The BSRI and gender schema theory: A reply to Spence and Heimreich. *Psychological Review, 88*, 369–371.

Berger, P. and Kellner, H. (1964) Marriage and the construction of reality. *Diogenes, 46*, 1–24.

Bernard, Jessie (1973) *The sociology of community.* Glenview, IL: Scott Foresman.

Bianchi, S.M. and Spain, D. (1983a) *American women: Three decades of change* (CDS-80–8). Washington, D.C.: Bureau of the Census.

———(1983b) *Wives who earn more than their husbands* (CDS-80–9). Washington, D.C.: Bureau of the Census.

Block, J. H. (1973) Conceptions of sex role: Some cross-cultural and longitudinal perspectives. *American Psychologist, 28,* 515–526.

Blumberg, Rae Lesser (1977) Women and work around the world. In Alice Sargent (Ed.) *Beyond Sex Roles* (pp. 412–433). St. Paul: West.

———(1978) *Stratification: Socioeconomic and sexual inequality.* Dubuque, IA: William C. Brown.

Blumstein, Peter and Schwartz, Pepper (1983) *American couples.* New York: Morrow.

Booth, Alan (1977) Wife's employment and husband's stress: A replication and refutation. *Journal of Marriage and the Family, 39,* 645–650.

Brannon, Robert (1976) The male sex role: Our culture's blueprint of manhood, and what it has done for us lately. In D. David and R. Brannon (Eds.) *The forty-nine percent majority* (pp. 1–45). Reading, MA: Addison-Wesley.

Broverman, I.K., Broverman, D.M., Clarkson, F.E., Rosenkrantz, P.S., and Vogel, S.R. (1970) Sex role stereotypes and clinical judgments of mental health. *Journal of Consulting and Clinical Psychology, 34,* 1–7.

Campbell, Frederick L. (1970) Family growth and variation in family role structure. *Journal of Marriage and the Family, 32,* 45–53.

Chafetz, Janet S. (1984) *Sex and advantage: A comparative macro-structural theory of sex stratification.* Totowa, NJ: Rowman and Allanheld.

Cook, Ellen Piel (1985) *Psychological androgyny.* New York: Pergamon.

De Beauvoir, Simone (1953) *The second sex.* New York: Knopf.

Doyle, James A. (1985) *Sex and gender: The human experience.* Dubuque, IA: Brown.

Durkheim, Emile (1933) *The division of labor.* New York: Free Press.

Feldman, Shirley S., Biringen, Zeynep C., and Nash, Sharon Churnin (1981) Fluctuations of sex-related self-attributions as a function of stage of family life cycle. *Developmental Psychology, 17,* 24–35.

Forisha, Barbara Lusk (1978) *Sex roles and personal awareness.* Morristown, NJ: General Learning Press.

Fox, M.F. and Hesse-Biber, S. (1984) *Women at work.* New York: Mayfield.

Gadlin, Howard (1977) Private lives and public order: A critical view of the history of intimate relations in the United States. In Howard Gadlin (Ed.) *Close relationships: Perspectives on the meaning of intimacy* (pp. 33–72). Amherst: University of Massachusetts Press.

Gagnon, J. and Simon, W. (1975) *Sexual conduct.* Chicago: Aldine.

Glenn, Norval and Weaver, Charles N. (1978) A multivariate multisurvey study of marital happiness. *Journal of Marriage and the Family, 40,* 269–282.

Glick, Paul C., Heer, D. M., and Beresford, J. C. (1963) Family formation and family composition: Trends and prospects. In M.B. Sussman (Ed.) *Sourcebook in marriage and the family,* 2d ed. (pp. 30–40). Boston: Houghton Mifflin.

Gould, M. and Kern-Daniels, R. (1977) Toward a sociological theory of gender and sex. *American Sociologist, 12,* 182–189.

Gronseth, E. (1972) The breadwinner trap. In L. K. Howe (Ed.) *The future of the family* (pp. 175–191). New York: Simon and Schuster.

Gutmann, David L. (1965) Women and the conception of ego strength. *Merrill Palmer Quarterly, 11,* 229–240.

Guttentag, Marcia and Secord, Paul (1983) *Too many women?* Beverly Hills: Sage.

Haug, Marie R. (1973) Social class measurement and women's occupational roles. *Social Forces, 51,* 86–98.

Hawkins, D.F. (1975) Estimation of nonresponse bias. *Sociological Methods and Research, 3,* 461–485.

Heilbrun, C.G. (1973) *Toward a recognition of androgyny.* New York: Knopf.

Hennig, M. and Jardim, A. (1977) *The managerial woman.* Garden City, NY: Anchor/Doubleday.

Hicks, M. W. and Platt, M. (1970) Marital happiness and stability: A review of research in the 60's. *Journal of Marriage and the Family, 32,* 553–574.

Hiller, Dana V. and Philliber, William W. (1980) Necessity, compatibility, and status attainment as factors in the labor-force participation of married women. *Journal of Marriage and the Family, 42,* 103–110.

———(1985) Internal consistency and correlates of the Bem sex role inventory. *Social Psychology Quarterly, 48,* 373–380.

Holmstrom, L. L. (1973) *The two career family.* Cambridge, MA: Schenkman.

Hood, Jane (1983) *Becoming a two-job family.* New York: Praeger.

Hornung, C. A. and McCullough, B. C. (1977) Status relationships in dual-employment marriages: Consequences for psychological well-being. *Journal of Marriage and the Family, 43,* 125–141.

Hornung, C. A., McCullough, B. C., and Sugimoto, T. (1981) Status relationships in marriage: Risk factors in spouse abuse. *Journal of Marriage and the Family, 43,* 675–692.

Houseknecht, S.K. and Macke, A.S. (1981) Combining marriage and career: The marital adjustment of professional women. *Journal of Marriage and the Family, 43,* 651–661.

Houseknecht, S.K. and Spanier, G.B. (1980) Marital disruption and higher education among women in the United States. *Sociological Quarterly, 21,* 375–389.

Huber, Joan (1976) Toward a sociotechnological theory of the women's movement. *Social Problems, 23,* 371–388.

———(1977) The future of parenthood: Implications of declining fertility. In Dana V. Hiller and Robin Sheets (Eds.) *Women and men: The consequences of power* (pp. 333–351). Cincinnati: University of Cincinnati Center for Women's Studies.

Huber, Joan and Spitze, Glenna (1980) Considering divorce: An expansion of Becker's theory of marital instability. *American Journal of Sociology, 86,* 75–89.

Jourard, Sidney M. (1971) *The transparent self.* New York: Van Nostrand Reinhold.

Juhasz, Joseph B. (1983) Social identity in the context of human and personal identity. In Theodore R. Sarbin and Karl E. Scheibe (Eds.) *Studies in social identity* (pp. 289–318). New York: Praeger.

Kennedy, D. (1970) *Birth control in America.* New Haven: Yale University Press.

Kimball, Gayle (1983) *The 50–50 marriage.* Boston: Beacon.

Komarovsky, M. (1973) Cultural contradictions and sex roles: The masculine case. *American Journal of Sociology, 78,* 873–884.

Kronenfeld, Jennie Jacobs and Whicker, Marcia Lynn (1986) Feminist movements and changes in sex roles: The influences of technology. *Sociological Focus, 19,* 47–60.

Kund, J. Helsing, Szklo, Moyses, and Comstock, George W. (1981) Factors associated with mortality after widowhood. *American Journal of Public Health, 71,* 802–809.

Kundsin, R. B. [Ed.] (1974) *Women and success.* New York: Morrow.

La Torre, Ronald A. (1979) *Sexual identity.* Chicago: Nelson-Hall.

Lenney, E. (1979) Androgyny: Some audacious assertions toward its coming of age. *Sex Roles, 5,* 703–719.

Lenski, Gerhard and Lenski, Jean (1982) *Human societies* (4th ed.). New York: McGraw-Hill.

Locksley, Anne and Colten, Mary Ellen (1979) Psychological androgyny: A case of mistaken identity? *Journal of Personality and Social Psychology, 37,* 1017–1031.

Lorber, Judith (1987) From the editor. *Gender & Society, 1,* 3–5.

Maslow, A.H. (1970 [1954]) *Motivation and personality.* New York: Harper and Row.

———(1971) *The farther reaches of human nature.* New York: Viking.

Mason, Karen O. and Bumpass, Larry L. (1975) U.S. women's sex-role ideology, 1970. *American Journal of Sociology, 80,* 1212–1219.

Mason, Karen O., Czajka, John L., and Arber, Sara (1976) Change in U.S. women's sex-role attitudes, 1964–1974. *American Sociological Review, 41,* 573–596.

Mead, George H. (1934) *Mind, self, and society.* Chicago: University of Chicago Press.

National Opinion Research Center (1986) *General social surveys 1972–1986 cumulative codebook.* Chicago: National Opinion Research Center, University of Chicago.

Nimkoff, M. F. and Ogburn, W. F. (1955) *Technology and the changing family.* Boston: Houghton Mifflin.

Nye, F. Ivan and Hoffman, Lois W. (1963) *The employed mother in America.* Chicago: Rand McNally.

Ogburn, William F. (1966 [1922]) *Social change.* New York: Dell.

Olds, L. (1981) *Fully human.* Englewood Cliffs, NJ: Prentice-Hall.

Oppenheimer, Valerie K. (1977) The sociology of women's economic role in the family. *American Sociological Review, 42,* 387–406.

Order, S.R. and Bradburn, N.M. (1969) Working wives and marital happiness. *American Journal of Sociology, 74,* 392–407.

Osmond, Marie W. and Martin, Patricia Y. (1975) Sex and sexism: A comparison of male and female sex-role attitudes. *Journal of Marriage and the Family, 37,* 744–753.

Parelius, A. P. (1975) Change and stability in college women's orientation toward education, family, and work. *Social Problems, 22,* 420–432.

Parsons, Talcott (1942) Age and sex in the social structure of the United States. *American Sociological Review, 7,* 604–616.

———(1943) The kinship system of the U.S. *American Anthropologist, 45,* 22–38.

Parsons, Talcott and Bales, Robert (1953) *Family, socialization, and interaction process.* New York: Free Press.

Philliber, William W. and Hiller, Dana V. (1983) Relative occupational attainments of spouses and later changes in marriage and wife's work experience. *Journal of Marriage and the Family, 45,* 161–170.

Pleck, Joseph H. (1977) The work-family role system. *Social Problems, 24,* 417–427.
————(1981) *The myth of masculinity.* Cambridge, MA: MIT Press.
Rapoport, Rhona and Rapoport, Robert N. (1971) *Dual career families.* Harmondsworth, U.K. and Baltimore: Penguin.
————(1975) Men, women and equity. *The Family Coordinator, 24,* 421–432.
Redfield, Robert (1947) The folk society. *American Journal of Sociology, 52,* 293–308.
Richardson, J.G. (1979) Wife's occupational superiority and marital troubles: An examination of the hypothesis. *Journal of Marriage and the Family, 41,* 63–72.
Ridley, Jeanne Clare (1972) The effects of population change on the roles and status of women: Perspective and speculation. In C. Safilios-Rothschild (Ed.) *Toward a sociology of women* (pp. 372–385). Lexington, MA: Xerox College Publishing.
Rothschild, Joan (1983) *Machina ex dea: Feminist perspective on technology.* Elmsford, NY: Pergamon.
Rubenstein, C. (1982) Real men don't earn less than their wives. *Psychology Today* (November), 36–41.
Rubin, Lillian (1983) *Intimate strangers, men and women together.* New York: Harper and Row.
Safilios-Rothschild, Constantina (1975) Family and stratification: Some macrosociological observations and hypotheses. *Journal of Marriage and the Family, 37,* 855–860.
————(1981) Toward a social psychology of relationships. *Psychology of Women Quarterly, 5* (Spring), 377–384.
Santos, R. (1975) The economics of marital status. In C. Lloyd (Ed.) *Sex discrimination and the division of labor* (pp. 245–268). New York: Columbia University Press.
Sarbin, Theodore and Scheibe, Karl E. [Eds.] (1983) A model of social identity. In *Studies in social identity* (pp. 5–30). New York: Praeger.
Scanzoni, Letha D. and Scanzoni, John (1981) *Men, women and change.* New York: McGraw-Hill.
Seidenberg, Robert (1973) *Marriage between equals.* Garden City, NY: Anchor/Doubleday.
Simpson, Ida Harper and England, Paula (1982) Conjugal work roles and marital solidarity. In Joan Aldous (Ed.) *Two paychecks* (pp. 147–171). Beverly Hills: Sage.
Singer, June (1973) *Boundaries of the soul.* Garden City, NY: Anchor/Doubleday.
Spake, Amanda (1984) The choices that brought me here. *MS.* (November), 48.
Spanier, Graham B. (1976) Measuring dyadic adjustment: New scales for assessing the quality of marriage and similar dyads. *Journal of Marriage and the Family, 38,* 15–28.
Spence, Janet T. and Helmreich, Robert (1978) *Masculinity and femininity: Their psychological dimensions, correlates and antecedents.* Austin: University of Texas Press.
Stacy, Judith and Thorne, Barrie (1985) The missing feminist revolution in sociology. *Social Problems, 32,* 301–316.
Statistical Abstract of the United States (1980) Washington, D.C.: Bureau of the Census.

———(1981) Washington, D.C.: Bureau of the Census.

———(1985) Washington, D.C.: Bureau of the Census.

———(1986) Washington, D.C.: Bureau of the Census.

Stiehm, Judith (1976) Invidious intimacy. *Social Policy, 6,* 12–16.

Stryker, Sheldon and Serpe, Richard T. (1982) Commitment, identity salience, and role behavior: Theory and research example. In William Ickes and Eric S. Knowles (Eds.) *Personality, roles, and social behavior* (pp. 199–218). New York: Springer-Verlag.

Sullerot, Evelyne (1971) *Women, society and change.* New York: McGraw-Hill.

Susser, Mervyn (1981) Widowhood: A situational life stress or a stressful event? *American Journal of Public Health, 71,* 793–796.

Taeuber, Conrad and Taeuber, Irene B. (1958) *The changing population of the United States.* New York: Wiley.

Tesser, Abraham (1980) Self esteem maintenance in family dynamics. *Journal of Personality and Social Psychology, 39,* 77–91.

Tesser, Abraham and Campbell, Jennifer (1980) Self-definition: The impact of the relative performance and similarity of others. *Social Psychology Quarterly, 43,* 341–347.

Tesser, Abraham and Smith, Jonathan (1980) Some effects of task relevance and friendship on helping: You don't always help the one you like. *Journal of Experimental Social Psychology, 16,* 582–590.

Toffler, Alvin (1980) *The third wave.* New York: Bantam.

Tonnies, Ferdinand (1957 [1987]) *Community and society* (translated from 1887 edition by C.P. Loomis). East Lansing: Michigan State University Press.

Unger, Rhoda Kesler (1979) Toward a redefinition of sex and gender. *American Psychologist, 34,* 1085–1094.

U.S. Bureau of the Census (1976) Fertility history and prospects of american women: June 1975. *Current Population Reports. Population Characteristics.* Series P-20, No. 288.

Virginia Slims (1980) *The 1980 Virginia Slims American women's opinion poll, a survey of contemporary attitudes.* Storrs, CT: Roper Organization.

Wall Street Journal (1982) Conflict at home: Wives of unemployed men support some families, but the cost to both spouses is heavy. December 8, 25.

Watson, Walter B. and Barth, Ernest A. (1964) Questionable assumptions in the theory of social stratification. *Pacific Sociological Review, 7,* 10–16.

Whicker, Marcia Lynn and Kronenfeld, Jennie Jacobs (1986) *Sex role changes, technology, politics, and policy.* New York: Praeger.

Willis, E. (1982) [letter] *MS.* (July), 181.

Wright, James D. (1978) Are working women really more satisfied? Evidence from several national surveys. *Journal of Marriage and the Family, 40,* 301–313.

Yankelovich, D. (1974) The meaning of work. In J.M. Rosow (Ed.) *The worker and the job* (pp. 19–48). Englewood Cliffs, NJ: Prentice-Hall.

Index

ABOUT THE AUTHORS

DANA VANNOY-HILLER is currently Professor of Sociology and Associate Dean for Academic Programs of the McMicken College of Arts and Sciences at the University of Cincinnati. She has co-authored with William Philliber many articles on dual-earner marriages and is presently studying the interrelation between adult development and family relationships.

WILLIAM W. PHILLIBER is currently Professor and Chair of the Department of Sociology at the State University of New York, College at New Paltz. He has co-authored with Dana Vannoy-Hiller numerous articles on dual-earner families, and he also writes on Appalachian cultural phenomena.

DATE DUE

MAY 1 0 1995			
NOV. 0 6 1997			
			Printed in USA